Roger
Love

Praise for *LOVE YOUR VOICE*

*"We teach our children lifetime healthy habits, such
as brushing our teeth daily, but we need to teach them one
more lifetime habit . . . and that is to do a few moments
of vocal exercises every day. By doing so, our voices will
never grow old. In this important book, Roger Love shows
us how to bring our voices to their optimal potential.
After doing the exercises for just a few days, I've already
removed traces of aging. I love Roger Love—he's brilliant.
Let him help you keep your voice vibrant and young!"*

— **Louise L. Hay,** the best-selling author
of *You Can Heal Your Life*

*"Roger Love has found a way to train the voice
and free the heart, mind, and spirit."*

— **John Gray,** the best-selling author of
Men Are from Mars, Women Are from Venus

*"Roger Love is a miracle worker. Let him change
your voice and the way that the world reacts to you."*

— **Glenn Beck,** author; radio and TV talk-show
host featured on CNN's *Headline News*

*"With Roger Love, you too have the opportunity
to learn from a truly amazing vocal master."*

— **Anthony Robbins,** motivational speaker; the best-selling
author of *Awaken the Giant Within* and *Unlimited Power*

"In politics, show business, or life in general, communication is the key to success. For anyone who wants to speak more effectively, Roger Love is the man to see."

— **Fred Thompson,** former U.S. senator; prosecutor; actor

"Roger . . . your unwavering support and confidence was the only thing that got me through vocally. Your spirit is truly infectious. Thank you for everything."

— **Sarah Michelle Gellar,** Emmy Award®–winning actress

LOVE
YOUR
VOICE

ALSO BY ROGER LOVE

Books
Set Your Voice Free
Sing Like the Stars!

Videos/DVDs
Get Out of the Shower!
Learn to Sing Like the Stars
Love to Sing

Audio Programs
The Perfect Voice
The Perfect Voice for Love & Relationships
The Perfect Voice for Money & the Workplace
Vocal Power: Speaking with Authority, Clarity, and Conviction

Please visit Hay House USA:
www.hayhouse.com®
Hay House Australia: **www.hayhouse.com.au**
Hay House UK: **www.hayhouse.co.uk**
Hay House South Africa: **orders@psdprom.co.za**
Hay House India: **www.hayhouse.co.in**

LOVE YOUR VOICE

Use Your Speaking Voice to Create Success,
Self-Confidence, and Star-like Charisma!

ROGER LOVE

HAY HOUSE, INC.
Carlsbad, California
London • Sydney • Johannesburg
Vancouver • Hong Kong • New Delhi

Published and distributed in the United States by: Hay House, Inc.: www.hayhouse.
com • *Published and distributed in Australia by:* Hay House Australia Pty. Ltd.: www.
hayhouse.com.au • *Published and distributed in the United Kingdom by:* Hay House
UK, Ltd.: www.hayhouse.co.uk • *Published and distributed in the Republic of South
Africa by:* Hay House SA (Pty), Ltd.: orders@psdprom.co.za • *Distributed in Canada
by:* Raincoast: www.raincoast.com • *Published in India by:* Hay House Publishers India:
www.hayhouse.co.in

Editorial supervision: Jill Kramer • *Design:* Tricia Breidenthal

Library of Congress Control Number: 2006937193

ISBN: 978-1-4019-1692-3

10 09 08 07   4 3 2 1
1st edition, August 2007

Printed in the United States of America

*This book is dedicated to
Miyoko, Madison, and Colin—
the only voices I could never live without.*

Contents

Introduction

The Missing Piece

My name is Roger Love, and I'm your new voice coach . . . and although I'm not claiming to have invented the wheel, I *have* spent the last 25 years working on one specific part of the human experience: *the voice.* I've coached superstars, politicians, billionaires, sports legends, preachers, teachers, supermodels, and supermoms and dads. As shocking as it may seem to you at this moment, I've learned that the voice is quite possibly the single most important tool you have to create real and lasting happiness and success. And although you probably don't realize it, *your voice could be ruining your life!*

"How absurd," you might say. "How could a *voice* matter that much?" My answer to that is simple: Life is all about communication. Research has proven that your level of achievement, happiness, and satisfaction is directly related to your ability to communicate. You can lose extra weight, develop killer abs, or look like a model on a magazine cover, but if you really want to *change your life,* one of the easiest ways to do so is to *change the way you sound*—and that's what this book is about.

When I work with famous actors such as Reese Witherspoon and Joaquin Phoenix, I'm fully aware that their voices are a big part of their success. When I coach money experts, including Suze Orman and Jennifer Openshaw, I know that their voices are helping them create a financial empire. When I teach Anthony Robbins, Louise L. Hay, John Gray, or Bill Phillips, I know that their voices are motivating hundreds of thousands of people and helping sell millions of books and audio programs.

My goal is to make *you* my next superstar client. That doesn't mean you have to get up onstage and speak or sing to thousands of people. I'm here to help you become the star of your own life. You and I are going to be partners in the greatest makeover you'll ever experience. It starts with your voice and then changes the way you feel—as well as the way others feel about you. By the time we're finished, you should be ready to take control of yourself and your relationships, job, and future. The voice is just our starting point. Once you and everyone around you love your voice, you'll be in a better position to take on the world . . . or at least your little corner of it.

Remember, whether you're living in Beverly Hills or in a trailer at the bottom of a hill, life doesn't exist without communication.

When you open your mouth and sound comes out, the people who hear it instantly start making value judgments about you: Are you rich? Intelligent? Powerful? Educated? Interesting? . . . Or are you a total bore and a waste of their time and energy? At that moment, *how you sound* is really all that matters.

Tonality Rules!

When it comes to important conversations, I believe that most of us spend way too much time worrying about *what* we're going to say. We've been mistakenly led to believe that the actual words we use matter that much, but the truth is that they hardly matter at all. How we sound is what is most important. For decades, research has shown us that the words we speak account for about 7 percent of a successful conversation.

Let me say that again: *The specific words you use are really not that important*—they only make up 7 percent of the whole picture. So regardless of what you say to someone, all the words in the world won't help you close the deal, get a date, make your children follow your instructions, or obtain the promotion you deserve.

So what accounts for the 93 percent? Well, 38 percent is determined by *tonality,* the way you sound when you open your mouth; and 55 percent is *physiology*, what your body is doing both internally and externally while you're speaking.

I've spent a great deal of my life learning the best way to utilize, understand, and teach people how to use tonality. The reason I've done so is because I believe it to be the most important communication tool you will ever possess. It's the missing link, the final puzzle piece, the Holy Grail. It will help unlock a door that leads to self-confidence, charisma, presence, popularity, and ultimate success. And the amazing thing is that it's all new and uncharted territory for you. You've probably never even thought about your voice in that way . . . never imagined that the key to achieving so much more was right there, literally on the tip of your tongue. But don't worry—I'm going to show you exactly what to do, step by step and sound by sound. And along the way, I'll also be giving you some advice on what you should and shouldn't be doing with your body—the physiological component.

When you master tonality and physiology, you'll end up with an amazing 93 percent of the whole communication picture. Knowing that it's all about the sounds you make, you'll be well on your way to becoming a winner. Your voice can turn into your new life-changing secret weapon, and I'm going to show you just how easy it is to achieve a powerful one. People who use their voices to make a living, such as famous actors, singers, radio personalities, motivational speakers, and politicians, are already aware of this secret . . . and now it's your turn to discover it.

I want to transform your voice into a moneymaking machine. Do you want to ask for a raise? I'll demonstrate how you should sound.

Are you looking to buy a new house or get a better apartment? Start packing! Want to ask that gorgeous guy or girl out tonight? Let me show you how. The world's most successful people use their voices to create amazing lifestyles, and now you can, too.

Judge and Jury

As I mentioned earlier, as soon as you start speaking, people are instantly making value judgments about you. There's no way around that—it's human nature to form an opinion of those you meet before you really get to know them. Understand that it's going to happen, and the key is to find a way of instantly making people perceive you in the way you wish to be perceived. You need to control the way others view you . . . and eventually the way you see, and feel about, yourself.

Let me explain this further. Let's say you have a particularly quiet speaking voice that's basically monotone—which means that you sound a bit like a piano with only two or three keys working. So when you speak to someone, that person is probably going to get the impression that you're shy, timid, emotionless, frail, and lacking personality. If you met Mr. or Ms. Right, you'd be instantly out of luck, going home alone again to a long night and a mediocre book. What would you expect that person to think? I already explained that the words you use don't really matter. If you *sound* shy, boring, and unexciting, why would other people think you're anything different? They don't know you. All they can base their judgment on in the beginning is how you sound and look and the way you make them feel.

You also need to realize how damaging and limiting other people's perceptions of you can be. If everyone around you gets the impression that you're weak and unassertive, they'll consistently act on that assumption and treat you accordingly. I believe that over time we all become a combination of what we think about ourselves and what other people think about us. We can't help but mold ourselves to fit the life that seems to unfold all around us. Stated simply, *we are what we believe we are and what others believe about us.* It's easy to be perceived as boring and shy and then become depressed and withdrawn from those people around you who see you that way. But on the flip side of the coin, there's the ability to change. Once your voice reflects the real you, others will react positively to you, and you'll feel better about yourself and your life.

But I'm Not a Professional Singer or Public Speaker!

Now I know that many of you might be thinking, *Hey, I'm not a big-time singing star or a public speaker who needs a voice coach! I don't have to be concerned about my singing voice, and I certainly don't have an audience to worry about!* Well, you might not be a singer or a professional speaker, but you definitely have an audience—everyone does. When you're at work, your audience comprises your boss, staff members, colleagues, and customers. If you're a parent, your audience is your children. If you're in a relationship, your audience is your significant other.

Yes, my friend, whether or not you realize it, you are an entertainer and a public speaker. If you open your mouth and sound comes out when anyone is listening, you're a public speaker, and whoever hears you is your public. We're all public speakers; it's just that some people are better at it than others. And as far as being entertainers is concerned, your audience is dying to be amused by you. Unfortunately, though, some of you are putting your listeners to sleep more quickly than a glass of warm milk and a *Tonight Show* rerun. But as I always say, "It's all about *sounds* . . . the ones you should or shouldn't be making." When you think about speaking, you need to remember that *people are listening,* and they do want to be entertained!

Star Quality: The Necessary Steps

In order to entertain the people who are listening to you, you need to be able to tap into your own star quality. Most of us don't usually think about star quality when we're trying to get a raise or a date or win an argument, but it's time we did. We live in a celebrity-style culture. We basically worship stars and place them high above normal folk. I want you to let me show you the same techniques I've given those stars . . . I want to help you be the star of your own life. It's my goal for people to think of *you* as a celebrity. Believe me, when that happens, your life will be a lot more exciting and you'll be that much closer to success and happiness.

The good news is, my experience has shown me that star quality has little to do with physical size, age, beauty, or even intelligence. It's actually a combination of unconscious and learned skills that give people the ability to create charisma whenever they want or need to. Acquire those skills and you can command the attention, loyalty, and enthusiasm of any audience—whether it's one other person or a crowd of thousands. In this book, using the same techniques I've taught to entertainment, media, and business celebrities, I'll show you how to focus your voice, mind, and body to create a star-like presence.

First, we'll work on making sure that your breathing is perfect. Then I'll teach you about the three main vocal ranges, including a secret voice many of you have never encountered. After that, we'll get to know which kind of voice you already have and what changes are necessary. I'll also teach you about the five building blocks of voice and how you can mix and match them to help you out in important situations. Then we'll work a bit on your physiology, as well as go over what you should and shouldn't be eating and drinking to achieve the perfect voice.

And remember, you don't just have my written words; the accompanying CD is also an invaluable guide and companion. You'll be able to read this book and hear my specific sound examples on the CD. It should prove to be a winning combination that leads you to complete understanding and mastery of all the material presented.

If I can make you sound, look, and feel like a star, the sky's the limit. I want people to get excited when you walk into a room or when they hear your voice on the phone. Once you can make that happen, you can reach out and grab the kind of life you want and deserve.

I'd also like to mention that the dramatic changes I have planned for your voice will take place almost immediately. My techniques are simple, so you won't have to spend the next year "fixing" your voice. I want you to follow along with this book and allow your voice to sound better with each and every page you read . . . it's that easy and that simple.

Nothing Is Impossible

Having taught for more than 25 years, I've seen and heard just about every vocal problem possible. Time and time again I've witnessed that with persistence, determination, and a genuine desire to change, anything is possible.

When Reese Witherspoon and Joaquin Phoenix came to me for singing help to prepare for the movie *Walk the Line* (Johnny Cash's life story), there was one big obstacle: Neither of them actually knew how. They were, however, willing to do whatever it took to make it happen. They spent every day with me for months doing vocal exercises, and then I took them into the studio and recorded all of the vocals for the movie and the soundtrack album. The film went on to be an incredible hit, winning Best Picture, Best Actor, and Best Actress at the Golden Globes®. Reese also won the SAG Award™ and ultimately the Academy Award® for Best Actress.

All of those awards honored a movie in which non-singers were playing singers. Hollywood and the public overwhelmingly agreed that they loved the singing and thought the stars' performances were amazing. If I can have that kind of success teaching nonprofessional singers to sing, just imagine how easy it will be for me to teach you to simply speak better than you ever imagined!

Almost Everyone Hates Their Own Voice

When people hear their own voices on tape, they're usually shocked by what they hear. Think about it: When was the last time you even listened to your own outgoing message on your voice mail or answering machine? If you haven't done so lately, I'd like you to play it right now and then ask yourself the following questions:

1. Did you like what you heard?
2. Would *you* go on a date with you?
3. Would *you* give you a raise?
4. Did you sound like a star?

Most people would answer each of those questions with a big *No* after listening to the garbled, nasally, monotone voice they just heard on tape. And sadly, that voice on your answering machine just happens to be what everyone else is listening to day in and day out. That voice is what's stopping you from making more friends, creating lasting relationships, getting a better job, and accomplishing the things you dream about.

Ignorance Is <u>Not</u> Bliss

So why haven't you done something about your voice until now? Maybe some of you have tried but were unsuccessful. I applaud you for your efforts and wish that you and I had hooked up sooner. It's not your fault that the techniques you may have tried previously didn't work. Perhaps it was just incomplete information or not your cup of tea. I truly believe that this time will be different.

If you've never thought seriously about your voice, don't feel bad. That's the norm. You didn't even know there was anything wrong. Like most people, you probably get up in the morning, croak out a few words before coffee, drive to work, and begin your day. Quite possibly the only time you stop and think about your voice is when you lose it. The day you wake up with laryngitis and can't speak any louder than a muffled, squeaky door hinge is the day you really think about the way you sound, and that's unfortunate. It's a sad but true fact that most of us go through our daily lives communicating with people, trying to achieve particular outcomes, and wanting to make the most of every day with sounds coming out of our mouths that are actually alienating everyone around us.

You might be the smartest person on the block, but that doesn't really matter if the people around you all think you're not that intelligent. You might have more personality than Robin Williams and be funnier than Chris Rock, but this won't help you if everyone you meet thinks that you lack a sense of humor. You need to always remember that people are listening, and that they're judging you based on the sounds that come out of your mouth . . . there's no getting around that. There is, however, a way to turn that information into a personal gold mine, a means of assuring that everyone sees you at your absolute best.

The easiest way to make that happen is to really listen to how you sound right now and then let me help you make the changes you need. There's no mystery or high level of difficulty here. You don't have to be a rocket scientist to transform your voice. I witness some of the most successful people in the world do it all day long. I can and will show you how easy it is to sound like the superstar you could be—and when that happens, your life will immediately change for the better.

So what do you say? . . . Are you game to try?

I promise you one thing: We're in this together now, and I won't give up on you until we reach our goals. I'm truly excited to have you along for the ride.

All my best,
Roger

How to Use
the Book and CD

The best way to use this book is to simply follow along with the text, listen to the specific audio examples on the bonus CD when directed to, and try whatever I ask you to do. For easy reference, you'll find a complete list of the tracks on the CD at the end of the book (see page 121). If you ever get a bit confused or aren't sure you understand something, feel free to go back over it until you get it. Everybody learns at a different speed. There's a trophy waiting at the end of this race for everyone, no matter when or how you cross the finish line. Don't try to rush through it all and miss important things that you need to learn. There's plenty of gold at the end of your rainbow, and no one is going to take it from you. All you have to do is stay on the path that I lay out for you.

After you've gone through the book and have listened to all of the audio examples and exercises, your new best friend is going to be the section of the CD called "Daily Warm-Up." I recommend that you practice it several times a week. I'd *love* it if you worked with it for at least 10 or 15 minutes every day. You can try it in the car on the way to work, in the shower, or while you're making breakfast. You can do it anytime you have a few minutes to spare.

Every day that you pop the CD in and warm up your voice, you're going to feel stronger; and more powerful, focused, confident, and successful. The exercises are designed to "trick" your vocal cords into the perfect positions to achieve great sounds. Have fun with them. At my studio here in Los Angeles, I try to fill every lesson with laughter and positive energy. It's a lot easier to learn things when you're having fun, and that's exactly how I've put together this whole program. I want you to enjoy our time together, along with your practice time away from me.

(**Note:** All females and young boys whose voices haven't yet changed through puberty should use the track on the CD labeled "Female Warm-Up." Males whose voices have already changed should use "Male Warm-Up.")

No Strain . . . All Gain

Make sure that when you practice the exercises on the CD, you never create any strain or pressure. If it ever hurts, you're doing something wrong. The lessons are set up to make your voice feel free and strong. It's not like weight lifting—you're not tearing muscles down to rebuild them stronger. You need to follow along with everything I say and every sound I demonstrate. I'm very aware of the specific places you could get into trouble or make a wrong sound choice, and I'll make suggestions whenever I think you could be getting too close to troubled waters. But no matter what I say, you need to stop yourself if you feel any discomfort at all. If you need to pause, just rest for a few minutes and then get right back to it. When you do, try to listen even more carefully and follow my lead.

A great voice is a goal worth achieving, and there's no reason at all that you can't enjoy every bit of the journey getting there.

Here's to your future . . . and to a voice that deserves to be loved!

CHAPTER ONE

Diaphragmatic Breathing

The Only Way to Go

In order for me to help you create an amazing voice, I first need to show you the best way to breathe. On a regular basis I'm quoted as saying, "Great speaking only happens when the right amount of air meets the right amount of vocal cord." And although that sounds a bit complicated, it's actually quite simple.

Air comes from your lungs and tries to get through your vocal cords and then out of your mouth. But the job of the cords is to temporarily hold the air back. When the pressure underneath becomes too much for them to handle, they separate and let a certain amount of air pass by, which is what creates the sounds you make.

To build your best possible voice, you need to have total control of that air. There's only one way to do this, and it's called *diaphragmatic breathing*. The problem is that most adults are just not used to breathing in that way . . . and please notice that I used the word *adults.* The reason I did so is to call attention to the fact that all babies—even you—were born doing perfect diaphragmatic breathing. That's right . . . when the stork dropped you off at your mom and dad's house, the hospital, or wherever you landed, you were breathing exactly as I want you to now. So all I have to do is refresh your memory and show you what you already knew.

Mirror, Mirror on the Wall

There are basically two types of breathing techniques: (1) diaphragmatic breathing, which I'll teach you; and (2) accessory breathing, which is mostly useless and a waste of time. But before we go any further, let's figure out which way *you* breathe. If at all possible, I'd like you to find a mirror that's big enough for you to see yourself from the waist up. If that's impossible right now, you can still do the following test.

Step 1

I want you to take a big deep breath in and try to be aware of what your chest and shoulders are doing. *Okay, let's do it now: 1, 2, 3 . . . breathe.*

When you inhaled, did you raise your chest and shoulders? Did your shoulders come up and try to visit with your ears? If so, that's called accessory breathing, and it's *not* what we're looking for. When you breathe like that, you're actually only getting a small amount of air into your lungs and are not gaining control of how that air goes back out again. For this reason, accessory breathing just isn't the way to vocal nirvana.

Step 2

Raise your shoulders way up to your ears and hold them there. Come on, keep them up. . . .

That doesn't feel very comfortable, does it? Now go ahead and let your shoulders go back down and relax. You should know that all day long when you raise your chest and shoulders every time you breathe, you're just begging for tension in your neck. I don't want you to create strain anywhere. Tension in your neck moves to your jaw, then to your voice, and pretty soon there's just way too much tension everywhere.

Step 3

Now let's focus on the second type of breathing, the one that will really work for you—diaphragmatic breathing.

Place your hand on your belly button and take a deep breath in. Pretend that you have a balloon in your stomach, and as you inhale, fill that area up with air without raising your chest and shoulders. The only place that should be moving is your abdomen.

Try it again with me now. Take a deep breath in through your nose, don't raise your chest, fill up the pretend balloon you have in your stomach, and then blow the air out of your mouth. Try that a few times and see if you can get used to it.

The Nose Knows

Did you notice that I asked you to breathe in through your nose? I did so because there are filters in your nasal passages that help moisten the air that moves through them. This is easier on the vocal cords and doesn't dry them out as much, which is important. If your vocal cords get dehydrated, they don't work as well and can get red and swollen. At that point, you might sound hoarse or even lose your voice.

Take a big breath in with your mouth wide open. Do you feel how all that air makes the back part of your throat dry? Now close your mouth, and take a big breath in through your nose. Do you notice the difference?

It's important to start being aware of whether or not you're a mouth breather. Do you usually wake up with a dry throat? Does it take you more than a few minutes to lose that "frog in the throat" morning sound? If so, you're probably already suffering the effects of being a mouth breather. You need to get used to inhaling only through your nose; it's a much better way for you to go.

The best place to start is simply to make sure that your mouth is closed when you inhale. The air has to get in somewhere—with your lips closed it will go in through your nose. Some people feel as if they can't get in a big enough breath because one nostril or the other is partially blocked. Well, to those people I say, "Welcome to the real world."

In all my years of teaching, I have perhaps seen three or four clients who could take in air through both nostrils at the same time without one being more blocked up. Most people are in the same boat that you and I are in. So don't think that just because your nose is a bit stuffy, you can't get enough air in that way. Great breathing is not about guzzling huge amounts of air; it's about comfortably bringing in just enough, using it to sound great, and then taking another breath and doing the same thing all over again.

With the breathing exercises I'm going to give you in this chapter, you should be well on your way to understanding and using diaphragmatic breathing in no time.

To Breathe or Not to Breathe

Let me get back to my main purpose in teaching you diaphragmatic breathing. As I've previously mentioned, I want you to control how the air flows out of your mouth. If you can do that, you'll be able to manipulate the sounds that come out with it. My goal is for you to create a solid, even stream of air that rides effortlessly out of your mouth. If I can get you to connect that bed of air with the words you speak, I can make you sound incredible.

You might ask, "Don't I already do that? Aren't the words already sailing out of my mouth on a proper bed of air?" Unfortunately, for many of you the answer is "No, they're not." Most of the time when you speak, the words and air come out in tiny bursts. That creates a small, shallow voice with a less-than-desirable tone quality.

My aim is to teach you how to take a diaphragmatic breath, letting your words ride out on that big, beautiful stream of air as you speak. It's important that we understand each other here: I only want you to speak when there's a solid flow of air out of your mouth and your stomach is coming back in.

You're Not a Fat Cat

If you've ever taken a yoga class or spent a few minutes at the gym with a qualified exercise trainer, your instructor may have mentioned diaphragmatic breathing and might have even gotten you to try it. The problem is, a lot of the time even the experts miss the most important part. They're so preoccupied with the inhalation (the way you breathe in) that they forget about the exhalation (the way you breathe out). To truly *love your voice* and have others feel the same way, you need to focus on the air coming out . . . that's where the true magic lies.

Have you ever seen anyone play the accordion? If so, do you remember how the player moved his or her hands apart and the instrument stretched? When that happens, air gets sucked into the accordion. Your body and lungs work in a very similar way: Just like the accordion, you also need to expand.

I want you to pretend that you just swallowed a big balloon. (Please don't actually do it! I have no desire to get calls from your lawyer, and no time to return them.) Every time you inhale, you need to let your stomach area come out as if air were filling up that balloon. You should also make sure that you aren't raising your chest and shoulders and creating physical tension.

When you let your stomach come out, you're suddenly in a wonderful position. By bringing your tummy back in, you can control how that air goes back out again, just like the accordion: When you want to get a lot of air out, you need to bring your stomach back in fast; when you only want a small amount, you should bring it in slowly. By breathing in this way, you're in a better position to regulate the air. You've found the accelerator pedal for your voice, and now you can control the speed. Together, we can use that new tool to make beautiful music together—the kind that only happens when you speak correctly.

A lot of people worry that by breathing diaphragmatically and letting their stomachs out, they'll end up looking fat. I fully realize that our culture has a preoccupation with washboard abs. And I do think that the exercise regimen and dietary guidelines that lead to that strong, flat stomach are fantastic. However, I believe that you can be in great shape, allow your tummy to come out far enough to get the right amount of air in, and still not look fat or unnatural. Most of the conversations you'll ever have will be face-to-face. In that position, it's almost impossible to see someone's stomach projecting out too much. People will be right in front of you, not staring at your belly from the side while you speak. Besides, when you breathe my way, you'll feel and sound better.

Let me give you a breathing exercise that will help you learn diaphragmatic breathing and make it a part of your everyday speaking life.

Breathing Exercise 1: The Accordion

Please try this with me. . . .

1.   Put your hand over your belly button.

2.   Take a breath in and let your stomach area come
      out as if you had a balloon inside.

3.   Remember not to raise your chest and shoulders
      as you inhale.

4.   Let your stomach come back in slowly as you
      recite the following words:

[Breathe in]
I want my stomach to slowly come in while I'm speaking.

[Breathe in]
The entire time I'm speaking my stomach needs to be coming in.

[Breathe in]
If my stomach is coming in when I speak,
I'm going to sound a lot better.

[Breathe in]
I need to breathe in through my nose, fill up my
abdominal area, and deflate my stomach when I speak.

Okay, good job! It's vital that you get used to your stomach coming in while you're speaking. It will get you so much closer to a better-sounding voice.

The Tension Trap

Aside from raising your chest when you breathe, the number one problem that prevents proper diaphragmatic breathing is tension at the top part of your stomach. The second that you grab and lock the muscles around your solar-plexus area, you're basically holding your breath and stopping it from getting out. I've already taught you that you *never* want to obstruct that air. The goal is to send a solid, even stream out of your mouth at all times while you're speaking. The words will then ride out on that air and create better sounds.

Some people think that if you hold your breath while you speak, you might actually get more words out and make longer sentences. But this is unnecessary—you're going to be taking thousands and thousands of breaths every day. You don't need to conserve air; it's not like a savings account that runs out of deposits. There's always more available to breathe in. The goal is to let the air ride out completely unobstructed and free of tension.

Think of the accordion again. You first need to separate your hands and get air into the instrument. Then, to actually make music, you have to bring the sides back together. When you stop the inward motion, the sound ceases. This is pretty much what happens with breathing. Whenever you prevent the stomach area from coming back in, the sound dies out. From now on, simply imagine that you have that accordion in your stomach. When you inhale, the accordion gets bigger, and when you exhale, it gets smaller again.

Breathing Exercise 2: The Slow Leak

As I've said before, airflow is a huge part of a great voice. Let me show you another breathing exercise you can practice.

1. Take a breath in through your nose and fill up your stomach area like a balloon.

2. With your teeth together and lips slightly apart, make a *sssssss* sound like the one at the beginning of the word *snake.*

3. With your hand on your tummy, let the smallest amount of air possible out of your mouth while you continuously make the *sssssss* sound. Draw it out for as long as you can.

4. Take another breath and try it to hold it even longer. Make sure that your stomach is slowly coming in without any tension.

Remember, the goal here is *not* to pass out. We're simply getting used to a little bit of air coming out and your stomach slowly falling back to its normal position. If you can *"sssssss"* for about 15 seconds on each exhale, you're doing great. The main purpose of *all* diaphragmatic-breathing exercises is simply to get you accustomed to your stomach coming out when you inhale, and back in as you exhale. That's all I'm concerned about right this second, and it's what you should be concentrating on, too.

Keep practicing your diaphragmatic breathing until it becomes second nature. I want you to breathe like this all the time, not just when you want to speak better. You'll need to check yourself every so often to make sure you're doing it correctly. Remember that great speaking only happens when the right amount of air is coming out of your mouth. Diaphragmatic breathing is the easiest way to make that happen. Your stomach has to be slowly coming in the entire time you're speaking—without that happening, you can never fully realize the true benefits of this breathing method.

In the next chapter, I'll discuss the vocal range, which is another important aspect of great speaking. We'll also learn about the secrets of the Middle voice.

CHAPTER TWO

Vocal Range: Chest, Middle, and Head Voice

The Secret Voice

I've spent most of my life talking about a secret part of the voice that hardly anyone else seems to recognize. I say to myself daily, "People—and especially all of the other voice coaches—are going to suddenly wake up and realize that they've missed a big part of the puzzle." But every day I continue to be amazed that it goes unnoticed.

The secret I'm talking about is called the *Middle voice,* and when you own it, it will help you create a new list of incredible sounds and take away any and all vocal pressure and strain. It will make it possible to go all the way up and down the range like a pianist playing a finely tuned instrument, connecting you to a myriad of beautiful sounds that your voice has never made before. It will put so many new tools at your fingertips that you'll be like a kid in a candy store rushing around and wanting to try everything. But before I demonstrate it, I'd like to explain a little bit more about my techniques and the things you'll need to know.

There are actually three main voices in the human vocal range:

- **Chest voice:** The low sounds at the bottom of your speaking voice

- **Head voice:** The sounds way above the normal vocal range

- **Middle voice:** A special sound combination that blends both the Chest and Head resonances together without creating a separation

As I said before, some people may have heard about the Chest and Head voices, but very few have been exposed to the magic of the Middle voice. I'm going to show you how to find it and add its amazing palette of sound colors to your own speech. When you own the Middle voice, you'll be that much closer to sounding fantastic.

Ultimately, my goal is to show you how to make all three voices strong, combining them together into one thick, powerful sound. By owning them all, you'll be able to draw on the lower, forceful, deep, rich, bassy tones; as well as the higher, brighter, pretty, trebly, bell-like resonances. And then by adding the edgy, strong, biting, goose-bumps-on-your-arms Middle sounds, you've got it made. People will love to listen to you speak. Having all three voices at your command will make you feel like you're the conductor of a well-rehearsed orchestra. The only thing I have to do now is show you how and where to wave your baton!

Let's Stay Connected: It's a Matter of Health

Most people get into all kinds of trouble when they try to go from the lows in Chest voice to the highs in Head voice. They find that their voice doesn't really know what to do. It breaks and cracks like a bad yodeler. This happens because they don't understand the concept of Middle voice.

Let me demonstrate the three voices for you now. Once you hear my examples of Middle voice, you'll begin to fully grasp exactly what it is and why it's so important.

**Please go to Track 1 on the CD
and listen to my demonstration.**

Chest voice only comfortably goes so high. The natural placement for the average speaking voice is in the lower part of the vocal range. As you listen to my demonstration, you'll hear exactly what it sounds like to bring your Chest voice up too far. You can create a lot of extra pressure that way. And all the squeezing together of the buttocks, furrowing of the brow, or tightening of the stomach can't make Chest voice go superhigh.

On the other hand, some people are actually trapped in their Head voice, and when they try to go down lower, it loses all of its strength and thickness. So Chest voice doesn't go high enough, and Head voice doesn't sound good down low. So what should we do? . . . The answer is that we need to also own Middle voice.

Why should you limit yourself to only one area of range? Would you want to be six feet tall and have all of the ceilings in your house set at that height? You wouldn't. It would be a lot more comfy to raise the ceilings to 20 feet, just in case you felt like standing on stilts and waving a big banner that said: "Listen to me."

There's another very important reason to own the Middle voice—it's actually good for you. Have you ever taken a yoga class and experienced the amount of stretching involved? If so, I'm sure you can appreciate that keeping your body relaxed and your muscles toned and flexible are both great ideas. Well, so it is with the vocal cords.

Most people are only making sounds that access a small portion of what the cords are capable of. By owning Middle voice, however, the cords end up getting a very special kind of exercise. Learning to go evenly from Chest to Middle to Head voice requires a great deal of physical strengthening and relaxation. The result is not only better sound, but an improved use of the entire vocal apparatus and musculature. I believe this to be the only true way to keep your voice in top-notch shape.

Battle of the Sexes: Let's Not Fight

It might help you to understand a bit more about what the vocal cords are actually doing in your throat.

Basically, they act as a filter for the air. Air comes out of the lungs and heads toward the cords, ready for a good fight. If the cords are closed, the air builds up pressure below them, trying to force them apart. The cords attempt to stop the air but always end up losing the battle—the pressure is too much for them to handle, so they open up and let some of the air pass through. As soon as that happens, they close back up again and get ready for the next fight. The air bursts that escape through the cords create the sounds we make when we speak or sing.

So many people are stuck making sounds they shouldn't. Do you know any men whose voices are unusually high? If so, they're probably using way too much Head voice. The reason why it sounds awkward is because we're not used to hearing men speak in this way, since they usually spend most of the time talking in

Chest voice. And what about women? If men are supposed to have a lot of Chest voice, are women supposed to sound feminine and speak in Head voice?

Nope . . . both men and women should use Chest voice as their primary speaking mode and then add Middle and Head voice as needed. And by the time I'm finished with you, you'll be able to do just that.

Who Wears the Pants?

While we're on the subject of women's voices, I want to give you an imaginary situation and ask you what you would do.

Let's say that you're a woman and you find yourself in a totally male-dominated business situation. There you are in the boss's office with men all around. You have an idea that you want them to hear, and you really need their support. If they like what you say, you could be in for a big raise. So, by trying to fit in—to be one of the guys—do you make your voice sound more masculine, lower, bassy, and more Chest voice heavy? Or do you go the opposite route? You're proud of being a woman and refuse to lower your voice until you sound like a man in a dress, so you let plenty of the Middle and Head voice croon out of your mouth, accepting the higher, prettier sounds as feminine and "perfect."

Do you know which is the right answer? If you said neither, give yourself a pat on the back . . . you're right. You should stop limiting yourself to either extreme. The reason why I teach everyone to have all three voices—Chest, Middle, and Head—is so that we can be free to own the entire range and combine the best of all three sounds into one incredible voice.

Some women have naturally lower voices. If that's you, great! But we'll be developing the Middle and Head voices so that you have complete command of the entire range. I'll just add whatever is missing in your voice until it comes out right.

Let's Exercise

To get you started, I'm going to give you your first Chest, Middle, and Head exercise. Just follow along with me and try to form whatever sound I ask you to. Make sure that you don't strain or create any physical discomfort—just have fun and keep an open mind.

This is the first of many exercises I'll offer you on the accompanying CD. Remember that by the time you're finished with the entire book and have gone through each one, you'll have a much better understanding of what's possible for your particular voice. And as I mentioned earlier, once you've read the book, you'll want to begin concentrating on the daily warm-up section of the CD. By doing so, you'll be building and strengthening your voice on a regular basis.

So let's get your feet wet.

Please go to Track 2 on the CD and perform the exercise that I describe.

In this chapter, I've shown you the three voices that are possible in the human vocal range and have explained the need for you to connect all of them. The next chapter will help you uncover what type of voice *you* actually have. Once you're armed with the knowledge of how you sound and have a system to modify what you don't like, you'll be in a better position to make positive changes.

CHAPTER THREE

Voice Types

Identifying Your Voice Type

Right now I'd like to spend a few minutes helping you identify what kind of voice you have. Even though everyone's is slightly different, there are basically only six major vocal types, and anybody who speaks is using some combination of them. Knowing which one you're closest to will help you figure out exactly what you need to change.

In my book *Set Your Voice Free,* I outlined these vocal types. If you've already read that work, I'd still like you to familiarize yourself with this chapter. My hope is that you'll be able to relearn some of the basic information as well as take advantage of newer insights that I'll share with you.

I've always believed that it's impossible to know what you sound like unless you make a recording of yourself and then listen to it. That's why you need to speak into a recording device every so often and keep track of your progress. If you have one handy, now would be a great time to pull it out. It will be very useful while you're working with the material in this chapter.

The Larynx

Before I get into the voice types, I need to show you how to use a very important little tool that you have in your throat—the larynx, or voice box, as some people call it. Being able to manipulate it a bit (which is something I'll teach you how to do) will really help get rid of the flaws and unwanted sounds in your voice.

Put your index finger on your chin and slide it backward down your throat until you get to the first bump . . . that's your Adam's apple, the front part of the larynx. Keep your finger on your Adam's apple and swallow. Feel how it goes way above your finger and then comes back down—that's good; it's supposed to do that. But that's *not* supposed happen while you're speaking. If the larynx comes up when you're trying to talk, it closes off the throat and makes your voice sound weak, small, tight, and restricted.

To find out if your larynx is rising too high when you speak, try this: Put your index finger back on your Adam's apple and start to speak out loud, saying anything you like. If it jumps above your finger as it did when you swallowed, that's too much movement. The larynx is only allowed to move up and down a little bit. If yours rose way up, we have to fix that. A high larynx is one of the most common problems affecting speakers, but it's very simple to get it back down to its proper position with a series of low-larynx exercises. Let me show you one now.

Please go to Track 3 on the CD and perform the exercise that I describe.

Now let's learn about the six vocal types.

Voice Type 1: The Nasal Professor

Please go to Track 4 on the CD and listen to my demonstration.

Do you sound at all like my demonstration? Do people ever say that you have a nasal voice? If so, practicing the exercise on Track 3 of the CD is the easiest way to reverse that problem. When you speak, put your finger on your Adam's apple and concentrate on keeping it down a little lower than usual. Add as much of the Yogi Bear, low-larynx sound as you need to stop your Adam's apple from rising—that way the larynx will stay where it's supposed to. After a while, it will just remain down by itself without the funny sounds.

Voice Type 2: The Rocky Balboa

**Please go to Track 5 on the CD
and listen to my demonstration.**

This voice happens when you block air from getting into the nose. Unless you currently have a severe cold, you probably don't sound exactly like my demonstration, but you might have a little bit of this vocal type mixed in.

It's entirely possible that there's a certain amount of either of the first two vocal types in your voice. You could be allowing too much air into the nasal-passage area, or not letting in enough. Either way, you don't have to worry. Nasality is a very common problem and it's easily fixable. All we need to do is reposition your larynx. To eliminate the Rocky Balboa sound, try the exercise on Track 6 and feel how it lets air vibrate into your nasal area.

**Please go to Track 6 on the CD and
perform the exercise that I describe.**

Voice Type 3: The Squeaky Hinge

**Please go to Track 7 on the CD
and listen to my demonstration.**

A lot of people might start out a sentence sounding smooth and even and then break into a voice that's too much like a creaky old door. I call this the "Squeaky Hinge," and a lot of the time it happens at the end of sentences because you're running out of air. Too much of this sound can actually give your voice a kind of dark and sinister vibe. If you use it all the time, it's about as appealing as nails on a chalkboard.

The Squeaky Hinge is also really tough on the vocal cords. It forces them to slam into each other without having enough air. It can make them red and swollen, and you can easily get hoarse and lose your voice.

If you hear any of this sound in your voice, I'd like to help you fix it now. The main problem is that you're still speaking after you've run out of air, which is why it usually happens at the end of a sentence. You need to make sure there's always enough air coming out of your mouth as you speak.

Hold your closed fingers up in front of your lips and tell me about what you had for breakfast. If you're speaking correctly, you should feel a steady amount of air hitting your fingers. If you don't feel anything or the air seems to start and stop, you need to work on that.

Do you remember how we already learned that the stomach should always be coming in while you're speaking? That's the easiest way to eliminate the Squeaky Hinge sound. After you get used to diaphragmatic breathing and practice the exercises at the end of the last chapter, the problem will cease to exist.

Voice Type 4: The Marilyn

**Please go to Track 8 on the CD
and listen to my demonstration.**

Do you remember the last time you saw a Marilyn Monroe film on DVD or TV? Can you recall what her voice sounded like? Let me refresh your memory: It was very airy, soft, breathy, and vulnerable. A lot of people seem to gravitate toward this vocal type. Maybe it's because they think it's sexy or appealing. Don't get me wrong—there are plenty of times I might use a little extra air or want someone to speak to me like that, but I think it's only effective in moderation and in specific situations.

Too many people use the airy, sexy thing all the time, thinking that it works for them. In reality, outside of the bedroom (or wherever you choose to get intimate), it hardly ever does. It certainly doesn't work in most business situations. If I were in a meeting with someone who spoke in that way, I could easily overshadow that individual and steal all the attention (and ideas) for myself. If there was only one promotion or raise up for grabs, believe me, after a few moments you wouldn't even remember that the other person was in the room.

Some people end up sounding breathy because they're overcompensating. Maybe earlier in their lives they were told that their voices were harsh, irritating, abrasive, or too loud. Perhaps one of their parents told them to shut up one too many times. They ended up swinging too far in the other direction to compensate and started talking with a whispery voice. The problem is that no matter how someone arrives at this way of speaking, it's not advantageous and is incredibly hard on the throat.

I always say that whispering is tougher on the vocal cords than screaming. When extra air passes by them, it dries up a lot of the natural moisture and lubrication they need. So I'd like you to keep in mind that while you may find a breathy voice inviting, laryngitis is really not that much fun. If you think it's the only way to sound sexy, gentle, or romantic, that's just not the case. There are many other beautiful sounds that are effective for seducing someone.

There are a number of exercises on the daily warm-up section of the CD that will help eliminate the excess Marilyn in your voice. If you practice them, you'll end up with the perfect mixture of air and cord—and it will become second nature sooner rather than later.

Voice Type 5: The Big Brass

Please go to Track 9 on the CD and listen to my demonstration.

Say the word *brass* and hold out the *aaaa* sound like I just did. When you do, you should hear a bit of what I call the "Big Brass." Some people have too much of that sound; and it makes their voices seem harsh, edgy, and somewhat irritating.

Brassiness happens when your vocal cords are vibrating fully, like the long strings of a piano. Most of the time that kind of vibration is great, but when the voice gets too brassy, it's because there isn't enough air coming through. Your body is actually swallowing up the sound before it comes out. In order to fix the Big Brass problem, you need to be certain that your larynx isn't going up. You can put your finger on your Adam's apple again and make sure that it stays down. You might also add some of the low-larynx, Yogi Bear sound I showed you before on Track 3 of the CD. By the time you've practiced for a week or so with the CD, your larynx will most likely stay down by itself.

Voice Type 6: The Husky Voice

**Please go to Track 10 on the CD
and listen to my demonstration.**

Called the Husky Voice, this vocal type is a lot less common than the other five, but I thought it was necessary to mention it anyway. Have you ever heard "What a Wonderful World" by Louis Armstrong? That song is great, but if you tried to speak that way on a regular basis, it would become grating and pretty unpleasant. This sound happens when the airy Marilyn voice and the Big Brass voice come together, and it makes the vocal cords extremely unhappy. When I demonstrate it for even a few seconds, my throat starts to hurt and I can feel my vocal cords getting dry and inflamed.

If you sound like this at all, you've probably gotten used to the tightening in your throat and the irritation of the cords. But I bet that you get hoarse a lot and probably lose your voice on a regular basis. If you hear even small traces of this quality in your voice when you listen to your voice on a recording device, you need to concentrate on two basic things:

1. Pay close attention to your breathing. Make sure you're letting your stomach area come out when you breathe in, and then allowing it to fall back slowly to its normal position as you speak.

2. Keep your larynx in its normal position. It shouldn't rise too high.

Don't Worry . . .

Just remember that the only reason we've been talking about the six basic vocal types is so you can identify them in your own voice. Unless you get better at hearing what you sound like, you will never have the voice you deserve and need. If you've already started to worry because you think you sound too much like the Nasal Professor or the Marilyn—or any of the other voice types—please remain calm. I promise that we'll fix any and all vocal problems together.

By the time you've finished this book and have started practicing the daily warm-up on the CD, your voice will be well on its way to sonic splendor. Whether or not you've identified your specific vocal type, your progress won't really be hindered. The techniques on the CD will alleviate any problems, one by one. Have a little faith, and remember that practice makes perfection infinitely more attainable.

The next chapter will give you the five vocal building blocks to play with. Using those blocks, you can tailor a voice that will help you achieve the goals you want and need, as well as create a voice that will be perfect in almost every situation you find yourself in.

CHAPTER FOUR

The Building Blocks of Voice

C'mon . . . Let's Play

One day I was working with a new student who admitted to having problems with his confidence level. I explained that he could either spend years in therapy working on his self-esteem issues or he could just learn to *sound* like he was the most assured person on the planet. You see, I have nothing against a quick fix, as long as it solves a real problem.

In these pages, I'm simply offering you an easier way to achieve many of the things you want and deserve. If you'd like people to think that you're the most confident person in town, start sounding as though you are. If you want everyone to believe that you're the smartest person at work, sound like you are! How you sound is how you're perceived by others. Just as a great chef combines ingredients to make the perfect recipe, loving your voice is about learning to mix and match certain sounds.

In order to do that, you need to explore the five building blocks of voice: *volume, melody, pitch, tone,* and *pace.* I've developed a simple system that allows you to measure all of these elements on a scale from 1 to 10 and decide how much of each to use when you're in specific situations. For example, if you want to ask for a raise tomorrow, how loud should you be when you speak to your boss? Say that you hope to ask your significant other to marry you . . . how much melody should you have in your voice? Or perhaps you've scheduled a noon meeting at the bank tomorrow and you really need a loan . . . how fast should you speak?

You'll learn how to manipulate these building blocks to achieve incredible things. I want every one of your conversations to end in success. Whatever *you* want, I want *for* you. How you sound is going to make all the difference in the world.

Volume

The first building block is *volume,* which is a huge key to sounding confident and secure. However, most people have no concept of how loud they should actually speak. I believe that we've become a society of whisperers, and for the most part, we speak way too softly. When students come into my studio, they're usually surprised by how loudly I want them to speak.

As I always say, "All speaking is public speaking." Whether you're talking to your mother, boy- or girlfriend, boss, teacher, or 500 people at a PTA meeting, you're still a public speaker. You need to learn to stop speaking as if you were talking to yourself. When other people are listening, you should achieve a certain level of volume. I tell people to pretend they're speaking to someone five to seven feet away from them.

I want your voice to fill up the space around you. No one should have to ask you to repeat what you just said or speak louder. The perception is that if you talk softly, what you have to say is really not that important. People might immediately think you're a weak person with no energy or charisma. And why would you want to give anyone that impression? Apart from whispering to someone you're sharing a pillow with, you ought to get used to speaking a lot louder.

What's Different about You?

Sometimes when I get students to speak louder, after they leave my studio to go back to their normal routine, their friends can get a little freaked out—they're not used to the extra volume. They're surprised that their buddy sounds different, so they say things such as "What's up with you? You sound weird. What happened to the old you?"

Believe me, this kind of experience happens a lot, and it's totally normal. It's all very simple: The people you hang around with get used to how you sound, the way you look, and what you say. If something changes, they're eventually going to notice. But that doesn't mean there's anything's wrong . . . it may actually mean that things are finally *right.*

We're all creatures of habit. We get accustomed to sounding a certain way even when it's bad for us and for those who hear us. That's why you need a little bit of courage to make big changes. Sooner or later, people will listen to the new you and hang on every word you speak. When your voice is right, you're never going to want to go back to the way you used to sound. Once you see how people react to you and treat you better—and notice how much better you feel about yourself—you'll be very happy you decided to make the changes.

Can You Cancan?

Now, I'm going to talk a bit more about volume and about how loud you should be. To achieve the perfect level of volume, you need to control two key variables:

1. The amount of air exiting your mouth
2. How thickly your cords are vibrating

Let's start with the air. Holding your fingers half an inch from your mouth, count from 1 to 10, getting louder as you go.

1 2 3 4 5 6 7 8 9 10

Do it again, and this time see if you notice more air hitting your fingers as you get louder. Play with it a few times and get used to it. As I've said before, you're supposed to feel plenty of air hit your fingers when you talk. If you don't, you're not loud enough.

Next, you need to make the cords vibrate in a thicker position. This means you're actually trying to engage the longest and thickest part of the vocal cords in order to create the strongest sounds. Say the word *can* and stretch out the *aaa* sound: *"caaaaaaan."* Do you feel the extra buzzing vibration in the back part of your throat? That's what it feels like when the cords vibrate more.

Great speaking can only happen when the right amount of air meets the right amount of cord vibration. Volume is not about increasing the air alone; if it were, then Marilyn Monroe would have sounded like she was screaming. And volume is not just about thick cords, either. Rather, it's all about finding the perfect *ratio* between the air and the cords. When the ratio is right on the money, you've hit upon the ideal volume.

As I told you before, I've attached a number scale from 1 to 10 for all five of the building blocks of voice. So let me demonstrate the scale for *volume.*

**Please go to Track 11 on the CD
and listen to my demonstration.**

1-2-3-4-5-6-7-8-9-10
Low----Normal----Loud

Melody

Okay, let's start with the basics. What is melody? Well, if you were to sit down at a piano and play a single key at a time in whatever pattern you wish, you'd be creating one. Melody is a string of notes that are attached to one another in any particular pattern. When a baby lies in a crib, the mobile plays a melody. When a new mother rocks her infant to sleep, the lullaby she sings has one, too. When you learn the alphabet, you do so with a melody. When you look for it, there's melody and music all around you. If you broke down the sounds, from the wind to the ocean, into their basic elements, they're all just melodies.

Now, some are better than others. For example, Beethoven was pretty good at coming up with melodies that would last for eternity, but the one in the song "(Shake, Shake, Shake) Shake Your Booty" might someday lose its "timeless" appeal. The good thing is, I'm not asking any of you to become a fabulous composer or a songwriter—that's not necessary at all. Melody as it relates to speaking is pretty easy to create.

Great speakers have discovered something singers have known for a long time: Melody can really bring words to life. Whether or not you realize it, you have melodies going on when you speak. It's just that some of them are totally boring and uninteresting. The trick is to learn to control them and use them to your advantage.

Songwriters and singers know that melody can move people emotionally. A great song might make you cry, dance, or remember a special moment in the past. There's no reason why you can't do the same thing to your audience just by speaking. If you want to get through to people, you need to stir their emotions. I'll show you how to use melody to create a memorable voice that people will love to listen to . . . I want your speaking voice to be music to their ears.

Don't Bore Me

Have you ever heard the word *monotone,* and do you know what it means? Well, when you look at a piano, you see that there are quite a number of black and white keys—the average piano has 88, to be exact. When you speak, there's a melody going on, a particular pattern of notes that are strung together underlying every word you utter. I call this *speak/singing.* I could listen to anyone talk and then go to a piano and find the exact notes that correspond with the ones they're speaking. The problem is, most people are creating really bad songs . . . they're speaking with almost no melody at all, as if there were only one note on their piano. That's what monotone is.

**Please go to Track 12 on the CD
and listen to my demonstration.**

If I spoke to you and only had one pitch going all the time—a single note that repeated over and over until you were about ready to burst with boredom or yell out for me to stop—that would be a good example of the word *monotone.*

I'm obviously exaggerating on Track 12, but it might surprise you to know that a tremendous proportion of the population actually speaks somewhat like this, and as far as I'm concerned, it's totally unacceptable. We need a lot more melody!

Checking You Out

Let's see if you can figure out how much melody you're using in your speaking voice right now. Pick up a book or a newspaper and record yourself reading any paragraph you like. As you play it back, listen specifically for how high and low you go. Does your voice swoop and soar up and down the vocal range, or does it stay on one note with very little variation? Listen back a few times if you need to. Put on your voice-coach ears and pretend that you're me. You don't need a master's degree in music to figure this out. Just concentrate on what you're listening for: melody or no melody.

I realize that it might be hard to discern whether or not you have enough. So let's just make it simple—I'm going to assume that you probably don't. Most people are way too close to monotone, and a little extra melody can never hurt. I'd really like you to experiment with adding a *lot* more to your voice. In the beginning, you might sound a little bit goofy, but that's all right. Eventually you'll stumble upon qualities that you like and want to incorporate into your everyday speaking. You'll get the best results if you spend time consciously exaggerating the highs and lows, moving into melody areas that you're not used to. I need you to go overboard with this, realizing that you will indeed scale it back later. Use your tape recorder again and try to speak with more melody. Then listen back and notice whether or not you're actually doing so.

My goal is to help you create a simple melody that underscores everything you say. The amount you use should keep your audience entertained, interested, and most important, wondering what you're going to say next. Think about it: People read novels from the beginning to the end. If they read the final pages first, they'd blow the surprise. And what about movies? A great film keeps the audience members on the edge of their seats till the very end. So why can't you use a bit of this magic when you speak? The answer is that you can—and melody is an easy way to make that happen. Here's how it works. . . .

Keep Them Guessing

If you speak using the same few pitches all the time, listeners start to get used to hearing only those notes. People don't need to have perfect pitch to realize that they're hearing the same note over and over again, so after a very short period of time—maybe 15 or 30 seconds—they think they already know which sounds will come out of your mouth next. When that happens, you're in real trouble, because if they think they know the sounds you're going to make, they start tuning you out and not listening at all. They imagine the words you're going to say before you utter them and then don't bother to pay attention. After all, if they already know the ending of the novel, why should they read the middle?

It's like listening to a broken record: It keeps playing the same sound over and over until it drives you crazy. After it skips seven or eight times, you don't expect that it's suddenly going to just fix itself and move on to the rest of the song. Remember that most people have incredibly short attention spans. If they think they already know what you're going to say, the conversation is pretty much over. The goal is to use melody as a type of variation tool and always keep them guessing. If my voice moves up and down like the melody to a great song, wouldn't you love to hear it almost as much as your favorite tune?

If you understand how to use melody, you can make your listener feel a certain way: happy, sad, hopeful, sorry, or any number of other emotions that might help you get what you want out of the situation. Remember that one of the reasons why you bought this book was to make changes in your life. If you can have some control over the way other people feel when they're around you and are listening to you, you're a lot closer to winning whatever prize your heart is set on.

I want you to get rid of the boring monotone voice you used to have once and for all, replacing it with one that's filled with excitement, variety, mystery, fun, and energy. More melody is a great way to start to make that happen. The daily warm-up on the CD will open your voice up to a cornucopia of new melodic possibilities.

Let me demonstrate the scale for *melody*.

**Please go to Track 13 on the CD
and listen to my demonstration.**

**1-2-3-4-5-6-7-8-9-10
Monotone--------------Varied**

Pitch

Is your voice too high or too low? Do you sound like Minnie Mouse or James Earl Jones? Setting your voice at its best pitch range will really help make sure that your voice sounds genuine and not artificial. It's always weird listening to people speak in a pitch range that doesn't seem to fit them—for example, Mike

Tyson has a high, childish voice. The good news is that as you speak, your voice naturally wants to fall into the right pitch range. However, you may have developed bad habits or made unconscious choices that have left you sounding funny or unnatural, kind of like you're wearing shoes that don't really fit.

I'll show you how to reset your voice to a more comfortable and natural place . . . one that shows off your personality, uniqueness, and charisma; helps get you hired; attracts the right relationship partner; and makes everyone want to hear what you have to say.

Pitch is very important in that strangers sometimes gauge your knowledge and intelligence by the pitch of your voice, at least until you can convince them otherwise. For example, let's say that you're working at a hardware store and someone asks you where the lightbulbs are. You don't want your voice to sound too high—like a child whose parent left him unattended—as the other person will instantly be taken aback by the high pitch and assume that you don't know where anything is. Sounding too low is also undesirable, because you'll come across as overly serious, making the customer feel as if he or she is imposing on you by asking the question. You want to have a pitch that makes the person sense that you're the expert. You need to sound like you know where everything is.

So how do you know what pitch to have when? By doing the daily warm-up and following along with the information in the rest of this book, it will all become second nature. However, it will speed up the process if you learn to control where your larynx is.

An Open Door

Pitch can be easily altered by making sure that your larynx is in the correct position. When it sits too high in your throat, your voice will automatically come out too high; if it sits too low, the pitch of your voice will usually be on the low side. The reason for this is simple: The position of the larynx determines the opening of the back part of the throat. When the larynx is down, more air is allowed to enter into the back of the throat and bounce around, creating a more open, bassy resonance. When the larynx sits too high, the air passageway is partially blocked. Less air gets through and it only has a small area to resonate in.

Imagine speaking in a large cathedral versus a small bathroom. The size of the room dictates how big and thick the sound becomes when it leaves your throat. The church will make you sound big and bassy, whereas the little bathroom will make you sound smaller and higher.

The easiest way to keep your larynx in the right position is to put your finger on it. When you speak, it's allowed to move up and down about a quarter to a half inch. If it moves up or down more than that, you need to compensate by adding a bit of the low-larynx sound I've demonstrated previously or taking some out. Remember that this isn't difficult to do. Pretend that you're a stereo with two knobs—one for bass and the other for treble. Just turn them and add or subtract whatever you need to keep the larynx from going up or down too much. If this makes you crazy, relax . . . I've already promised you that the exercises on the CD will make everything right. Just have faith and practice.

**Please go to Track 14 on the CD
and listen to my demonstration.**

**1-2-3-4-5-6-7-8-9-10
Low-----Mid------High**

Tone

The tone of your voice is determined by the amount of airy or edgy sounds you make. When there's too much air, the tone gets too wispy and fragile—the way Marilyn Monroe used to speak. This "bedroom voice" might work great when you're in a horizontal position or are in the mood to get intimate with someone, but the downside is that you can also be perceived as being less intelligent . . . that is, a bit of an airhead.

I do believe that a certain amount of airiness can be useful in suggesting that you're friendly and accessible, but it can easily undermine your intent or credibility. In general, I think that the really airy voice is a bad choice for getting the most out of your life. I don't want the people who are listening to be able to just brush you aside as if you were powerless. I want them to stop, take you seriously, and realize that you have incredible strength and passion. I don't think that's possible when you speak with too much airiness.

At the other end of the spectrum is the harsh, edgy sound that you hear when you hold out the *a* sound in the word *brass.* It's an aggressive and sometimes irritating tone, but in the right proportion, it makes your voice more powerful and substantial. Again, let me stress that the tone of your voice will also fall into its proper place when you practice the warm-up. Every day that you do so, your voice will be creating the perfect balance between air and vocal-cord vibration. That's how I'm going to make sure you end up with the perfect tone balance for your voice.

Here is my demonstration of the 1–10 scale for *tone.*

Please go to Track 15 on the CD
and listen to my demonstration.

1-2-3-4-5-6-7-8-9-10
Airy----Normal----Edgy

Pace

If you've ever been hustled by a fast-talking salesman or sat there waiting for a slow speaker to get to the end of a sentence, you know how strongly pace can affect you. Too fast, and you feel like you're being run over; too slow, and you start to think the speaker is not only slow, but also as dumb as a doorknob.

So what's your tempo saying about you, and how is it affecting what your listeners are hearing and thinking about you?

First, keep in mind that everybody operates at a different pace. If you're jittery and restless, your metabolism is probably naturally set on high: You walk fast, eat fast, and talk fast. On the other hand, you may be a low-key, calm person who rarely gets overly excited and hates to be rushed. Your heartbeat and breathing are probably slower, and your blood pressure is likely lower.

You need to be able to tune in to your natural speed. Recording yourself and playing the tape back should really help with this. You need to think about whether or not you talk more quickly or slowly than the people around you. Spend some time listening to your friends and co-workers and notice how your pace compares with theirs. There's no absolute good or bad speed, but I'd like you to become aware of what happens when your tempo is slower or faster. I need you to try to pay attention to how your conversations go when you're speaking at different speeds, and then you can see whether or not it's helping you achieve your desired results.

Another good way to determine the proper pace is to see if listeners are constantly interrupting you. If they are, you're probably speaking too slowly. If they ask you to repeat parts of what you said, you're most likely speaking too fast.

The Need for Speed

When you get nervous or excited, it's quite normal for the pace of your voice to go into turbo drive. You might be fine one-on-one or in familiar situations with people you trust, but when you step in front of an audience or have to give somebody bad news—or have unbelievably *good* news and you're bursting at the seams to share it—sometimes adrenaline kicks in and increases your pulse rate. At that moment, if you can't find a way to calm yourself back down, more likely than not the words will just rush out too fast. As you feverishly try to get them all out, the sound of your voice can really suffer. You could end up losing all of the great melody you already learned how to create and fall into a kind of drone-like monotone voice instead.

If you're rushing through the sentences and not giving yourself time to breathe, there's no way that your voice is going to create the best sounds possible. Believe me, this isn't the voice you want to use to tell your boss that you need next Friday off or let your spouse know that there's a huge dent in the new car.

I'd like you to play with pacing when you talk. You might start by picking up the newspaper or a book and reading into your recording device. Read a sentence or two at your normal speed, and then change the pace. Slow down for another sentence or two and then speed up again. What speed do *you* think sounds the best? Which one makes you sound energetic or powerful or loving? You might notice that different content seems to be more effective at different speeds.

Play with it. If you're a fast talker normally, try slowing your pace on every other phone call at work. How do people respond to you? When you're face-to-face with a friend, watch for cues. Are you connecting better when you slow down? Or does a certain amount of speed help get your message across?

In Slow Motion

When you speak too slowly, you also run the risk of distorting your voice and sounding lazy. Have you seen any old John Wayne movies lately on cable? Well, when I imitate that voice, I think it makes me sound weak, tired, and a bit dim-witted. In many situations, listening to a slow speaker who frequently pauses makes you question the person's credibility. The pauses suggest hesitancy or lack of authority, or imply that the individual just hasn't figured out what the heck he or she is trying to say. The slow-talking speaker can also seem unprepared or inarticulate, even though that might not be the case at all. But honestly, what good is being the sharpest tool in the shed if everybody around you thinks that you're dense? My goal is to make sure that you always create the best impression possible.

How Do You Sound?

There's no magic pill for fixing the pace of your speech other than just listening and adjusting, listening and adjusting. Use your recordings for feedback. Keep in mind that different situations require a variety of paces. If you're a therapist, for example, you might want to provide lots of space in your speech pattern to encourage the other person to respond. If you're a firefighter, you probably need to speak a bit faster so that your instructions are heard and carried out before the building burns down. Just play around with pace and try to make sure it's appropriate to your particular circumstances. The good news is that your listeners will quite often let you know by asking you to stop talking so fast, or by telling you that you're boring them to death!

So, here's my demonstration of the 1–10 scale for *pace.*

**Please go to Track 16 on the CD
and listen to my demonstration.**

**1-2-3-4-5-6-7-8-9-10
Slow----Normal----Fast**

It's Not Rocket Science

I've done my best to break down the voice into only five building blocks. I'm constantly working toward teaching the maximum amount of information in the simplest way, with the shortest number of steps. I've never believed that the voice was a magical, unknowable instrument lurking mysteriously in the shadows under our chin or that we needed to be rocket scientists to figure out how to operate it. Instead, I've spent a great deal of my life writing and rewriting the manual to help make it more accessible and controllable.

By thinking in terms of pitch, pace, melody, tone, and volume, you can easily create the perfect voice for yourself. In the next chapter you're going to take the building blocks you've just learned and relate them to specific situations you might encounter. You'll figure out just what sounds to use when and where.

CHAPTER FIVE

Vocal Profiles

The Combination Plate

So far you've been working very hard to make sure you have all the tools you need to create an amazing voice. I'd like to spend the next bit of our time together talking about specific situations you either have encountered or will encounter in the course of your everyday life, along with how to get the most out of each of them. Using the building blocks you learned earlier—volume, tone, pitch, pace, and melody—you can figure out the best way to succeed on a daily basis.

As I've said before, the way you communicate is directly linked to your level of success in life. Time and again, I see that those who make it to the top have somehow created a vocal personality that helps them. Successful people have managed to create a voice that actually helps them achieve what they want and need out of life. Is there a single perfect voice? No. But there is a perfect voice for *you,* one that combines who you are, who you want to be, and what you're all about.

For a number of years, I've been teaching one of the world's most famous motivational speakers, Anthony Robbins. Tony has coached everyone from Presidents to top sports athletes. He also has a very unusual-sounding voice: It's a unique blend of power, thickness, edginess, and forcefulness. If he was somebody you were speaking to at the dry cleaner's, you could potentially be frightened or intimidated by the sounds he makes. But when he's onstage with 10,000 or more people in the audience, he becomes charismatic and powerful enough to help you change your life for the better. Tony's voice is perfect for his message—he wants to shake you out of the dull, boring life you've been living and challenge you to take serious action and create the incredible life you deserve. If he sounded sweet, shy, or loving all the time, he wouldn't have the same impact on the crowd.

Okay, so you don't have any immediate plans to speak in front of 10,000 people. Still, you and I need to continue working to find the sounds that are best for you, your job, your relationships, and your purpose in life. That's what this book is all about: It's a way to help you discover more possibilities so that you can gain more control over your life and the special situations you find yourself in.

I'd like to look at a few basic career types and some specific situations, showing you how I might mix and match sounds to create the right voice for each one. I call this *vocal profiling.* Feel free to go back and reread the chapter on the building blocks of voice or listen to the CD demonstrations I did if you need a refresher or you get confused.

Vocal Profile 1: Cashier

Let's say you work at a bank or some other financial institution or you're a cashier at a retail establishment and you spend a lot of time dealing with money. You're going to need a voice that's a blend of strength, knowledge, security, compassion, and persuasion. If you sound too airy, too hesitant, or not smart enough, the customers will never have confidence in what you say to them. When people are dealing with money, they need to feel safe. So let's do a little vocal profile.

— **Volume.** You have to be a little on the loud side without making customers feel that they're being shouted at. Remember that there might be a certain amount of activity going on all around you, especially if you're working at a big store. You need to get just above the rest of the noise in order to be heard. A **6** on the volume scale should be fine.

1 2 3 4 5 **<u>6</u>** 7 8 9 10
Soft---------------Loud

— **Pace.** You don't want to rush. You can't make people think that you're steamrollering them into making a choice about what to do with their money. A steady pace is best—not too slow, not too fast. A **5** or **6** will work.

1 2 3 4 **<u>5 6</u>** 7 8 9 10
Slow---------------Fast

— **Melody.** You don't want too much melody. Customers need to think of you as a money expert, not an out-of-work musician. Try a **5**.

1 2 3 4 **<u>5</u>** 6 7 8 9 10
Monotone------------Varied

— **Pitch.** I want you to stay on the lower side of the pitch range. Sounding like Minnie Mouse right now will only make you seem young and inexperienced. When people deal with money, they want to feel as if they're doing business with someone as solid as the Rock of Gibraltar. They need to hear sounds that are strong and on the lower side of the pitch range. A **4** will work nicely.

1 2 3 **4** 5 6 7 8 9 10
Low----------------High

— **Tone.** You want to have a steady stream of air coming out, but you don't want to sound airy at all. I metioned before how people perceive someone with an airy voice as an airhead. When that happens, although they might be inclined to kiss you, they definitely don't want you to handle their precious money. They need to be sure that you're very serious and professional. Use a **6** or **7**.

1 2 3 4 5 6 **6 7** 8 9 10
Airy---------------Edgy

**Please go to Track 17 on the CD and
listen to my demonstration of the Cashier.**

Vocal Profile 2: Salesperson

What if you have a job where you need to sell something? It could be cars, homes, electronics, or housewares. Whatever it is, you need a voice that instills security, compassion, knowledge, patience, understanding, loyalty, and insight. You want the buyers to feel that they're dealing with a caring expert who will gladly spend whatever time is necessary to make sure they purchase the perfect thing. They should trust and like you or you won't make the sale. Nobody wants to buy something from a jerk, no matter how cheap the price is.

— **Volume.** You should maintain a slightly louder than average volume level, but be careful not to make the people think that you're shouting at them. You need to be confident yet courteous. Like a good therapist, your job is to listen to what they have to say. That way, you can make an educated guess as to what you should sell them. Try a **6** or **7**.

1 2 3 4 5 **6 7** 8 9 10
Soft---------------Loud

— **Pace.** You need to slow yourself down here. Don't let the excitement of making a sale force you to speed up. Keep an even speed and become the voice that calms others' fears. Go for a **4**.

1 2 3 **4** 5 6 7 8 9 10
Slow---------------Fast

— **Melody.** You need to have a strong amount of melody. It will give your listeners the feeling that you have a great deal of imagination and creativity—that you can see past what is and help them discover what could be. Use a **7** or **8.**

1 2 3 4 5 6 <u>**7 8**</u> 9 10
Monotone------------Varied

— **Pitch.** Stay in the lower third of your voice, your Chest voice. Even though you're using a lot of melody, I want everyone to think that you're grounded, solid, and connected to the earth. Use about a **4** here.

1 2 3 <u>**4**</u> 5 6 7 8 9 10
Low----------------High

— **Tone.** You can actually have a tiny bit more air in your voice than you normally would. I want people to feel as though you're their best friend and they have nothing at all to fear from you. They should think that you're the sweetest, most knowledgeable person they've ever met. Try a **4** or **5.**

1 2 3 <u>**4 5**</u> 6 7 8 9 10
Airy---------------Edgy

**Please go to Track 18 on the CD and
listen to my demonstration of the Salesperson.**

Vocal Profile 3: Doctor's/Dentist's Office Employee

If you work in a doctor's or a dentist's office or any other similar medical or health-care business, your voice needs to be a blend of good bedside manner, compassion, insight, and calmness. Each word ought to sound caring, knowledgeable, and at the same time maybe even a little bit technical.

The patients who come into an environment where they're worried about their health or need to feel hopeful and secure that they're in a place with people who can help them get better. If you walked into a doctor's office and were greeted by someone behind the counter who had an extremely nasal voice, would you want that person to get really close to you? I don't think so. You'd be too afraid that you would catch whatever the employee had. On the other hand, if the assistant sounded like Yogi Bear, you might think that he or she was kind of slow or dim-witted and imagine that the doctor might be just as goofy.

— **Volume.** Keep your volume right in the center of the scale. I want you to leave the impression that no matter what happens, you'll stay constant, consistent, and steady.

1 2 3 4 **5 6** 7 8 9 10
Soft---------------Loud

— **Pace.** I want you to speak a bit more quickly than normal and give people the sense that you're a genius and therefore your brain works faster than theirs. The extra speed will help with that. Try about a **7.**

1 2 3 4 5 6 **7** 8 910
Slow---------------Fast

— **Melody.** Patients want their doctors, nurses, and medical personnel to be miracle workers. They expect them to be all and know all and still have time to see them. Extra melody will show them your "superhero/bigger than life" attitude. Try a **7** or **8.**

1 2 3 4 5 6 **7 8** 9 10
Monotone---------------Varied

— **Pitch.** You can go a bit higher than you normally do. I want you to give the impression that you're reaching for the stars to find the answers to listeners' medical questions. Use a **6** or **7**.

1 2 3 4 5 **6 7** 8 9 10
Low----------------High

— **Tone.** It's all right to have a bit more edge in your voice. You'll still have a nice bedside manner with the extra melody, but the edge will provide a no-nonsense atmosphere. Try a **7**.

1 2 3 4 5 6 **7** 8 9 10
Airy--------------Edgy

**Please go to Track 19 on the CD and
listen to my demonstration of the Doctor's Office.**

Vocal Profile 4: Teacher

If you're a teacher or a caregiver who's responsible for making sure someone or many people learn specific information, you're going to need a voice that commands attention and is strong, self-assured, knowledgeable, and compassionate. Your goal is to teach your students with a firm attitude and an open heart. You want to be partners in the learning process and have them trust you, follow you, and be excited by all the possibilities of a new day. Your voice becomes a key factor in making all of that happen.

— **Volume.** You'll need a bit more volume than usual to make sure all of your students can hear you above whatever else is going on in the room. Your volume should show them that you mean business. Don't worry about seeming like you're shouting or being a bully. Once you mix a great deal of melody into the sound, the students will only think of you as a kind and loving helper. Try a **7.**

1 2 3 4 5 6 <u>7</u> 8 9 10
Soft---------------Loud

— **Pace.** The key is to create an even pace that allows people to follow you without getting bored or thinking about anything else. You want to go slightly faster than you would normally. That way, you're presenting the information in a way that challenges the students to keep up with you. It tells them that you have faith in their ability to learn quickly, and that you believe they're smart enough to follow along with you at that pace. Use a **7.**

1 2 3 4 5 6 <u>7</u> 8 9 10
Slow---------------Fast

— **Melody.** I'm going to be looking for a very high level of melody in this situation. A great teacher needs to have an incredible personality and present a world of knowledge in an exciting way. Such an individual ought to be entertaining, colorful, charismatic, and brimming with energy and life. There's no room on the planet for a teacher who's dull as dirt. How can you expect students to pay attention to a person who doesn't excite them or command their attention?

A teacher needs to exude confidence, be larger than life, and offer students a wonderful journey they'll never forget. Like being on a great ride at an amusement park, they want to have fun with someone who *is* fun. Extreme melody is the perfect way to create that type of atmosphere. Try an **8**.

1 2 3 4 5 6 7 <u>**8**</u> 9 10
Monotone---------------Varied

— **Pitch.** Even though I want you to have a great deal of melody, I don't think you should go too high up the vocal range. In order to come across as powerful and strong, I advise staying slightly lower in pitch. A student is not going to take you seriously if you sound like Minnie Mouse. A teacher should be a pillar of strength who is both solid and steadfast. Staying on the lower side of the pitch range will help you appear that way. Try a **4** or a **5**.

1 2 3 **4 5** 6 7 8 9 10
Low----------------High

— **Tone.** The airy thing needs to fly out the window if you're a teacher. You can't expect anyone to be mesmerized by your every word if you sound light and airy. Even though you still want to sound compassionate, you have to do so in a stronger, more confident way. The goal is to convince students that you're the most intelligent person in the universe. The minute they feel that they're smarter than you, you've already lost the battle.

You'll end up getting plenty of the warm and fuzzy sounds by having an extreme amount of melody—you won't need to resort to the airy voice to achieve them. I don't want your students to feel that they can just push you over with a feather or bully you into giving them a better grade than they deserve. If you sound airy, it gives them the impression that they can manipulate you, which prevents you from creating the perfect atmosphere and maintaining control. Try a **7.**

1 2 3 4 5 6 **7** 8 9 10
Airy---------------Edgy

**Please go to Track 20 on the CD and
listen to my demonstration of the Teacher.**

Vocal Profile 5: Receptionist/Phone Salesperson

A wonderful receptionist can become the voice of an entire company. When you call a business and speak to a representative, you can't help but form an impression of the whole organization based on what that person sounds like. If he or she seems nice, intelligent, helpful, and concerned, you begin to feel more at ease and satisfied that you've called the right place. If the person sounds angry, frustrated, or less than intelligent, you can't help but start to feel impatient and irritated and actually lose confidence in the company as a whole. After all, a business is only as good as the people who work there. If the first person you speak to sounds less than competent, why should you think the rest of the company would be any different?

And if you're selling something over the phone, the same rules apply. You need to sound bright, attentive, knowledgeable, friendly, professional, and cheerful.

— **Volume.** No matter how much money the company might spend on a great phone system, the equipment still has a lot of limitations. Whether you use a headset or a regular handheld phone, it can only handle so much volume without distorting the sound of your voice. Therefore, I'm looking for a solid, even volume that's slightly on the lower side of the spectrum. If you're too loud, the individual on the other end of the line simply pulls back and becomes guarded. People aren't interested in a bulldozer running over them—they want to be given information in a secure and positive way that isn't overpowering or threatening. Use about a **5** or **6.**

1 2 3 4 **5 6** 7 8 9 10
Soft---------------Loud

— **Pace.** You lose a great deal of ability to influence others over the phone, since you don't have the benefit of being with them in person. They can easily shut you off by hanging up or simply taking the earpiece away from their ear. Holding their attention becomes much more difficult, which is why I want you to concentrate on a pace that's slightly faster than normal.

You only have a very short time to make sure the other person becomes interested. You already have a lot going against you due to all of the boring, pushy telemarketers who call during dinnertime trying to sell things that are absolutely unwanted. Most people are afraid to answer the phone if they think it's just going to be someone they don't know wasting their precious time. Therefore, you need to speak faster than you normally do to get to the point before you lose your audience. Try a **7.**

1 2 3 4 5 6 <u>7</u> 8 910
Slow---------------Fast

— **Melody.** One of the easiest ways to show confidence and personality over the phone is to have a lot of melody. Remember that your listeners can't see the bright red dress you're wearing or the supercool jeans that make you look like a rock star. They can't observe your new hairdo or your fabulous smile . . . but they can imagine all of those positive things about you. They can dream that you're the best-looking guy or girl on the planet.

It's your goal to make them believe that you're all that and more, no matter what the reality is. You could be the most ordinary person in the world, but if you sound like a winner, you've captured their imagination and gained a few more minutes of their time. That could be all you need to influence them or get them to buy something you want to sell. Melody is the perfect way to give the impression that you're the most interesting person around. Try an **8.**

1 2 3 4 5 6 7 **8** 9 10
Monotone-------------Varied

— **Pitch.** In order to keep a certain amount of energy going, I want you to speak on the slightly higher side of the pitch range. Remember that you have a very short time to impress the person on the other end of the phone and need to make sure that he or she doesn't get bored quickly. Speaking a little higher will complement all the extra melody you have going on and also keep the energy up. Try a **6** or **7.**

1 2 3 4 5 **6 7** 8 9 10
Low----------------High

— **Tone.** I'm looking to add a bit more air in than normal—but only combined with a solid, thick amount of vocal-cord strength. In other words, I don't mind a little extra soothing air sounds coming out of you as long as there's still a strong underlying vocal resonance and quality that creates the foundation. I don't want you to seem like a piece of dust floating in the wind. I'd simply like you to add a nice amount of air to a solid, pure voice to help make you sound a bit more user-friendly and approachable. Try a **6** or a **7.**

1 2 3 4 5 **6 7** 8 9 10
Airy------------------Edgy

**Please go to Track 21 on the CD and
listen to my demonstration of the Receptionist.**

Asking Your Boss for a Raise

In today's world, getting a raise is no easy feat. So many com-
panies have scaled down and cut back that a lot of people I know
are just happy to have a job. Still, living expenses keep getting
higher, and the new health-insurance premiums seem like a king's
ransom.

A raise might not solve all your problems, but it could certainly
help out. To make it happen, you'll need a voice that sounds powerful, insightful, indispensable . . . and of course, more expensive.

— **Volume.** The goal here is to make sure that you sound confident and secure without seeming pushy or bossy. You should be
assertive without being threatening. One major piece of this puzzle
is volume. I want you to start out with a strong impression, so be
louder than normal. Let your voice fill the room with solid, resonant
sound. You need to initiate the conversation and take control of
the meeting. If your boss does, he or she may try to begin with a

lot of excuses and/or history about the company and its current financial woes. It's better for you to make the opening move.

During the dialogue, never let your voice get softer. It's a sign of weakness and creates the illusion of giving in or retreating. Keep your volume up, and never back down from what you believe to be fair compensation for your hard work. Try using a **7.**

1 2 3 4 5 6 <u>7</u> 8 9 10
Soft------------------Loud

— **Pace.** The speed of your conversation should be like a Ferrari in second gear. I want you to be on the slower side of normal. Your boss needs to hear every syllable you utter. The slower speed will emphasize each word and show that you're thoughtful, careful, and even-tempered.

Don't rush! Your boss will think that you're afraid. When you speed up, it implies that you're nervous. You obviously don't want to give that impression. Like a dog that senses fear in humans, the boss will pick up on your anxiety and have less confidence in you. That's why you need to stay at a constant pace and never let him or her fill any large pauses in the conversation with anything that might get in the way of achieving your ultimate goal. Go for a **4.**

1 2 3 <u>4</u> 5 6 7 8 9 10
Slow------------------Fast

— **Melody.** I'm suggesting that you use a lot of melody, because the more creative you are, the more money you deserve. Extra melody makes you sound exciting and innovative and therefore worthy of being paid more.

The boss needs to hear music when you speak. You want people mesmerized by the sound of your voice. Using a lot of melody, going up and down with tasteful finesse, is a great way to influence others and succeed. Go for the **8**.

1 2 3 4 5 6 7 **8** 9 10
Monotone-------------Varied

— **Pitch.** Stay in the lower third of your range. I want the extra thickness and richness that comes from that area. I'd like you to sound powerful and strong and let the low frequencies vibrate your boss's body. When you go too high, it gives the illusion that you're frightened and fragile, like a boy going through puberty. Let the low, vibrant sounds make your boss realize that you're unstoppable and unwavering in your commitment to achieving a positive outcome. Try a **3** or **4**.

1 2 **3 4** 5 6 7 8 9 10
Low-------------------High

— **Tone.** An airy, fragile, sensitive voice will not work in this situation. You don't want to come across as being easily manipulated. You need to be much more edgy and bright with regard to tonality. It's important that your words cut right through the space between you and the listener, getting deep into his or her ears, mind, and heart. I don't want your voice or your message to dissolve in the air as it leaves your mouth. Keeping your voice clean, clear, edgy, and focused will make your boss more attentive to you and what's really important. A **7** should work nicely.

1 2 3 4 5 6 <u>7</u> 8 9 10
Airy-------------------Edgy

Asking Someone Out on a Date

Now let's look at a situation that's always freaking people out: asking someone out on a date. Whether you're in love or lust, the goal is the same—you want the person to say yes. In order for that to happen, you have to make sure that you're perceived as completely desirable and unforgettable. Whether or not the person is looking to hook up with you, or anybody else for that matter, isn't important at this point. You still want him or her to think that you're the best thing since sliced bread. There's no harm in the person doing a little daydreaming about you, even if he or she can't follow through on those desires and impulses.

One of the fastest ways to make all this happen is by finding the right voice for the situation. Remember that if this person has never met you, he or she has no preconceived notions about you. You have no excess baggage or bad history. The slate is completely clean and ready to be written on. And the fact is, you can never give someone a first impression more than once, so you don't want to blow it. What he or she initially thinks about you is either going to make or break you when it comes to your potential for actually getting the date. The other person has no idea whether you've already broken dozens of hearts or had *your* heart broken dozens of times. All he or she knows is the reality you help to create with the right voice.

— **Volume.** The goal here is to achieve a volume level that makes the other person stop whatever he or she is doing and listen to you. Many times both sexes are trying so hard to be polite or respectful that they approach each other in a shy way with a low volume level. That hardly ever works. It's too easy for someone to just dismiss you and look away if you don't immediately command attention.

A little extra volume is a crucial element in this game. I'm not talking about being obnoxious and loud—I'm simply looking for a volume that will cut right to the heart of the other person, even if there are a multitude of distractions all around. Remember that volume is only one of the elements. Alone, it offers nothing special . . . but if it's used with the right combination of the other vocal ingredients, you might have a chance with the object of your affection.

I'm suggesting that you stay around the middle of the scale. That way you'll come across as commanding without actually barking out commands. Try a **6**.

1 2 3 4 5 <u>**6**</u> 7 8 9 10
Soft-----------------Loud

— **Pace.** A little slower is always better in the beginning stages of any relationship. Even the word *relationship* signifies that a certain amount of time has passed. People don't talk about the one-night stand they had last night as a relationship. Even though you may be only interested in a date, you need to show the other person that it's worth his or her while to invest a bit of time in you. You have to make him or her want to roll the dice and gamble on a potential huge prize at the end: *you.*

In a world that's filled with people rushing from one place to another and not stopping to smell the roses along the way, don't fall into the trap of talking too quickly. Speak on the slower side without coming across as a moron who can't connect enough words together to make a good sentence. Try to stay around a **4**.

1 2 3 **4** 5 6 7 8 9 10
Slow------------------Fast

— **Melody.** With the volume up and the pace slow, I'm count-ing on melody to be your big secret weapon. It's important for you to be perceived as an incredibly interesting, vivacious, bigger-than-life, smart, funny, and attractive person. That's a long list of positive traits to fit into a few moments. Still, melody is the fastest way to get that across. A lot of melody makes you sound happy, fun, intelligent, creative, and mysterious . . . all at the same time. Use about an **8** on the scale.

1 2 3 4 5 6 7 **8** 9 10
Monotone-----------------Varied

— **Pitch.** In this instance, I still think that it's important for you to stay on the lower side of the pitch range. No matter your gender, I want you to sound strong and confident, as if you don't need the date to complete you or the incredible life you already have going. So try to stay around a **4.**

1 2 3 **4** 5 6 7 8 9 10
Low----------------High

— **Tone.** This part of the voice is a bit trickier. The last thing I want you to do is come across as an airhead/Marilyn Monroe type or a frat boy/surfer dude. Still, there ought to be just a hint of an airy quality—that way you sound as though you're focused but have graciously taken a bit of the edge off. You're still a wild animal, yet for the next few minutes you're going to just purr like a kitten. Afterward, however, the claws just might come out. . . . My suggestion is to stay around a **4** or **5** on the tone scale.

1 2 3 **4 5** 6 7 8 9 10
Airy------------------Edgy

Is Any of This Making You a Fake or a Phony?

I want you to understand that I'm doing everything I can to make sure you never sound fake, phony, or artificial. Even though this vocal-profiling system might seem a little calculated or manipulative right now, it's really just an easy way to get you to a place where everything that escapes your mouth sounds totally natural.

The bottom line is that all day long sounds are coming out of your mouth, and you're either benefiting or suffering because of them. If anything, I'm trying to get you in touch with the better parts of yourself . . . I just want to help you put your best foot forward. Think of the profiles as a simple way to get you focused on the different building blocks of voice and how you should be thinking of using them.

As I mentioned before, great chefs have to know all of the separate ingredients that make up their signature dishes. Mixing them together perfectly is their way of showing their culinary expertise. All you're learning to do is combine your vocal ingredients so that you end up looking like the best thing on the menu. If you practice, I promise that all of this will become second nature to you—just keep playing with it.

A Little Something to Remember

The vocal profiles are simply a starting point. I want you to be thinking about pitch, pace, tone, melody, and volume, and the many possibilities they represent, so that you realize just how important these elements are. In the beginning of the book, I explained how the words you use account for only about 7 percent of a successful conversation. I also explained that the tone of your voice was responsible for a whopping 38 percent. In order to take full advantage of the implications of that statistic, you need to have an open mind—and all five of the building blocks of voice. Don't think about the vocal profiles as though they were carved in stone and brought down from the mountain by Moses. Think of them as something I created to spark your imagination and broaden your vocal creativity.

In the next chapter, I'm going to begin a discussion of physiology and tell you how you can add its wonderful benefits to the new and vocally improved you.

CHAPTER SIX

Physiology, Hand Gestures, and Body Movements

The Power of Physiology

In the Introduction, I told you that 55 percent of a successful conversation has to do with physiology—what your body is doing while sound is coming out of your mouth. The way you stand, breathe, gesture, and walk, as well as what your eyes do and the expressions on your face . . . all this and more counts as physiology. I'd like to offer you a few simple tips to help you understand how important proper physiology is, and how you can make it work to your advantage.

The good news is, you don't have to look like Brad Pitt or Jennifer Lopez to come across as appealing, charismatic, powerful, entertaining, and desirable. So much comes down to the way you sound and how you use your body.

"Blue" Eyes

Have you ever noticed that when you're really sad, your face starts to frown, and that if you ever cry, it's virtually impossible to smile at the same time? That's because it's difficult to separate emotions from physiology. How you feel is usually written all over your face and body like a billboard on the street. Think about it: If I had you look at a group of individuals, don't you think you'd be able to pick out the ones who were depressed or sad? I think you would. They'd probably be the people with bad posture and sad eyes. They'd be moving more slowly than the rest, speaking more softly, and looking older than they actually are.

The happy people in the group would have their chests up and their shoulders back and down, and they'd be moving energetically and walking briskly. They'd be smiling a lot, and their faces would look younger than their actual age. This isn't exactly rocket science, and I'm not a psychic. I simply know that the way people feel is easily readable if you just take the time to look closely and listen. And whether or not you realize it, people are observing *you* and forming opinions based on the way you sound and move.

Way Off Broadway

Let's start out with something easy: how you should and shouldn't be moving your hands when you speak. You could have a lot of great things to say, but you might be guilty of a common problem that's bringing you down—I call it _parallel gestures,_ and it's basically when you use both hands in exactly the same way at the same time.

Instead of slicing the air with one hand to emphasize a point, you do so with two. Everything one hand does, the other mirrors exactly. If you point your index finger at someone, the same finger on the other hand is simultaneously pointing. And even though you see people on TV such as Presidents, politicians, entertainers, and newscasters doing it, they're all making themselves look physically uncomfortable.

The effect is actually comical, although of course it's not intended to be. If I were in front of you right now making parallel gestures, you'd soon get the feeling that you and I were stuck in a terrible off-off-Broadway musical. When you speak to people, the goal isn't to make them feel as if they're a trapped audience and you're a bad performer. Your intent is to make them sense that you're totally comfortable with your body and with being in front of them. Parallel gestures make it hard to accomplish that.

In the course of a normal conversation, our hands are supposed to move independent of each other. We might lift a hand and then let it drop, or point with one hand while the other does something totally different. Let me explain why that's more natural.

It's a No-Brainer

Did you know that each side of the body is controlled by the opposite side of the brain? Well, you do now . . . and guess what? Our gestures should obviously reflect that. The left side of the brain tells your right hand where and how to move, and the right side of your brain is telling your left hand the same information. That's how the brain and body work together. It's the reason why you walk the way you do, one foot in front of the other, moving from one side of the body to the other, instead of hopping like a kangaroo.

Medically speaking, the left and right hemispheres of the brain don't usually send identical messages to both sides of the body at exactly the same time. That's why I say that parallel gestures aren't a natural thing. People who use them look uncomfortable and appear to be disconnected from their bodies. This kind of movement can easily create a barrier between you and your listeners. If you look uncomfortable, the people listening to you sense it and start to feel sympathetically uneasy with you. When that happens, they don't want to watch or listen to you.

Are You Guilty?

To find out how guilty you are of overdoing parallel gestures, try this: Stand in front of a mirror that's big enough for you to see yourself from the waist up. Talk about anything you want, it doesn't matter what. Describe the first time you went Rollerblading, ice-skated, played basketball, or fell in love. Remember that to get an honest read on this, you have to force yourselves to *do* a lot of hand gestures. If you talk with your arms at your sides, it really doesn't tell you what you need to know. Okay, go ahead and try it.

Did you notice what your hands were doing? Were they mirroring each other or moving differently?

Now go back and try it again, but this time when you see yourself making a parallel gesture—that is, when both hands are in the same exact position—stop for a second where you are and then let one hand drop or move it up . . . just change something. Continue speaking until you find yourself making another parallel gesture. Stop again, switch one hand's position, and then continue speaking. This simple mirror work will increase your awareness and let your body know that you're on to its little unconscious habit. Notice the gestures and then stop using them—it's really that simple and doable.

Plane Parking

Let me give you a few more points on hand movements and physiology. First, I don't want those you're speaking with to be afraid of getting hit in the face by your over-the-top hand motions. Some people just wave their hands around as if they're directing airplanes where and where not to park. If you're one of those heavy-arm-waving types, you need to learn to tone that down. You have to get more personality and emotion from your speaking voice instead of from your hands and arms. You can use *sounds* to get your points across, not extra hand movements. Most of the time all those big, overdone gestures only draw attention away from what you're actually saying. When you unintentionally force people to focus on your hands and arms, they can't concentrate on *you*. Whenever you don't know where to put your hands and arms, just drop them to your sides. They can stay there and look comfortable for quite a while before you need to move them at all.

I also want you to avoid crossing your arms while speaking. It sends a closed-off signal to anyone watching you, as if you're somehow done with them and have no more interest in the conversation, or you have something to hide. You always want to appear confident and open. Crossing your arms definitely gets in the way of that.

Mouth Positions

The next part of your body I want to talk about is your mouth. And although I love seeing happy, grinning faces just as much as the next person, there's a special little problem that happens when you speak and smile at the same time. So let's do another little exercise to check the position of your mouth when you talk. You can look into the same mirror you've been using so far or find any small hand mirror lying around the house.

Start to recite the alphabet slowly and watch what the corners of your mouth are doing as you move from letter to letter. When you reach the letters *E* and *G,* do you see your mouth becoming wider and the corners moving out as if you're forming a smile?

When some people speak, they unknowingly allow their mouths to go into a wide, smiley position on a regular basis, but that's not a good thing for your voice. Let me explain why. When you smile and let the corners of your mouth go wide, the sound gets directed toward the nasal cavity. If you don't smile, it has a much better chance of vibrating inside your cheeks and picking up a richer, warmer tone.

A lot of people object very strongly when I ask them not to smile and speak at the same time, but it really does make the voice sound flat, nasal, and less appealing. My advice is to use this facial expression at the points when it will do the most good and get you what you really want. There's plenty of time to smile before and/or after each and every sentence you speak, if that's what you choose to do. Just don't exaggerate the smile thing while you're saying words.

To correct a too-wide habit, try this:

1. Put an index finger on either side of your mouth.

2. Push your lips in just a bit so that they're slightly pursed.

3. Start to recite the alphabet again or talk about what you're doing for dinner tonight. As you speak, don't let your lips go any wider than their starting position— just keep the corners of your mouth in.

With a little practice, you can easily stop your mouth from going too wide when you speak. The payoff for doing so is substantial. You'll love the rich tones this adds to your voice, and you'll notice how dramatically any brassiness fades. It's a very quick way to make your voice sound infinitely more appealing and less harsh.

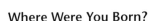

Where Were You Born?

I appreciate all accents in their natural habitat. Sometimes, however, when you take an accent or regionalism away from its place of origin, it can create a few potential problems of perception. That's why you might want to avoid some accents in certain situations. One of the easiest ways to do so is to control your mouth position. When you let the corners of your mouth widen, you can end up distorting the sound of many of the vowels, which is a big part of what accents are made of.

Try saying "Park the car" without smiling. Now make a big grin and say it again. Hopefully you just noticed how the vowels changed and you suddenly sounded like you were born and raised in Boston. Just by changing your mouth position, you traveled to New England and all you did was smile.

What about the Queen's English? I was lucky enough to have a mother who grew up with the sound of Westminster. Her beautiful speaking voice soothed and calmed me throughout my life. If you don't already have such an accent, let me show you how to simulate one now. If you take the word *not* and pronounce it with the corners of your mouth in a normal position, it comes out "not." However, if you pushed your lips out as if you were about to say *"Oooo"* and then kept them there as you said the word, you'd sound a lot more British. Please try it and see what I mean.

As I said before, all accents can work. You just need to be aware that you *have* one and make sure that it's working for you, which is why I suggest that you pay attention to any time you use the wide, smiley mouth, and avoid doing so too much. I understand that many people just have a naturally wide mouth position. If that's the case with you, you can still learn to push your lips out a bit when you speak. This will force the corners of your mouth to come in a bit, assuming a more natural-sounding position. It might take a while, but you'll get used to it.

Posture

Aside from looking strong, comfortable, and in touch with your body, one of the main reasons why posture is so important has to do with making sure that you have an easy way for the air to get into your lungs.

So please try this:

1. Stand up straight, with your feet about shoulder width apart.

2. Roll your head around to ease any tension in your neck.

3. Hold your head level with your chin parallel to the ground, not tipped up or down.

4. Raise your chest up and bring your shoulders back and down. This position really helps your rib cage move out of the way so that the air moves easily into the lungs, which is exactly what you want.

Slumping, or rounding your shoulders slightly forward, collapses the rib cage and makes it a lot harder to get the right amount of air into your lungs. Let me show you what happens to the voice when the rib cage gets in the way:

1. Start with good posture, keeping your chest up and your shoulders back and down.

2. Count slowly from one to ten and start to round over your shoulders a little at a time as though you were doing a sit-up motion.

3. As you get farther and farther down, notice how your voice begins to close up.

I don't want your voice to close up and sound shallow, as you just demonstrated. That's why I'm so determined to make sure that you have good posture.

There are tons of books written about posture, but for our purposes, all I really want you to think about is keeping your chest up and your shoulders back and down. It's important that you don't let your torso come up higher when you inhale and collapse down lower as you exhale. When you have good posture, your chest and shoulders aren't supposed to move at all when you breathe. The only part of your body that changes position should be your stomach going in and out, as you hopefully recall from the time we spent earlier working on your diaphragmatic breathing.

In this chapter, I've briefly discussed the idea that physiology is a huge part of effective communication. I want you to keep track of your posture, your mouth positions, and your hand movements.

And speaking of hand movements, the next chapter will help you decide which foods and drinks you should and shouldn't pick up and put into your mouth.

CHAPTER SEVEN

What to Eat and Drink

Nourishing Your Voice

Whether or not you realize it, what you eat and drink has a lot to do with keeping your voice in perfect shape. And to make things worse, most of the old wives' tales that you've heard are totally untrue. Every day, all around the world people are eating and drinking things that are supposed to be good for their voices, and in truth they're creating more problems for themselves. Let me explain why I say that.

This Is No Tea Party

When I was a kid, every morning my mom used to wake me up with a cup of tea with honey and lemon. She thought that it would be good for my throat. It wasn't until years later that I realized her good intentions were actually making my throat and voice worse. When I tell people that tea with honey and lemon is bad for their voices, they usually look at me as if I were crazy. But truthfully, tea usually has caffeine in it, and that creates extra-thick, unwanted phlegm—the yucky stuff you're always trying to clear *out* of your throat.

If you're a coffee, tea, or soda drinker, you've probably already noticed that you need to clear your throat a lot. That's because caffeine acts as a diuretic, which means that it flushes water out of your system. The loss of that fluid makes the phlegm in your throat thicker and more concentrated. Are you one of those people who needs coffee or tea every day to survive? If so, I'm not going to stand between you and your morning cup of joe. One or two cups won't really hurt you that much, but I strongly advise you to stop there and switch to decaf, herbal tea, or water for the rest of the day.

Now let's talk about the lemon in tea. First, it makes you salivate more than normal, which also creates too much of the extra-thick phlegm. As a matter of fact, all citrus has a tendency to produce excess amounts. So if you know that you're going to have an important conversation, you don't want to fill up on OJ, grapefruit juice, or lemonade anytime prior. Clearing your throat isn't a very sexy sound, and besides, every time you do, the vocal cords get a bit more red and irritated.

Then there's the temperature issue of many beverages. Whenever you drink something that's too hot or cold, it can change the size of the tissues it comes in contact with. The funny thing is, it can even change the size of tissues it *doesn't* directly come in contact with. What if you were hired to be a hand model: Would you take a steaming-hot bath right before the photo shoot? No, because your hands would look like prunes as soon as you got out of the water. When it comes to keeping your vocal cords happy and healthy, the last thing you want to do is make them change their size. When the liquid is too hot or cold, that can happen.

It's a little bit tricky, but when you drink something, the liquid goes down one hole in your throat. The vocal cords live down another. So it's basically impossible to drink or eat anything and have it come in direct contact with the vocal cords. But extremely hot or cold beverages can still bother them and make them irritated. Any temperature change of adjacent tissues—or, for that matter, of tissues anywhere in the body—can affect the delicate mucous membranes of the vocal cords, causing them to dilate or contract. If that happens, your voice is never going to sound perfect.

I Drink to You

So what's the number one thing you can eat or drink right now to keep your voice in great shape? That's easy: more water. There's nothing in the world that makes your voice happier than water. I'd like it if you drank a half a gallon of it a day. I'd *love* it if you drank even more than that. And I don't mean the kind that just happens to be in your coffee or Coca-Cola; I mean actual, pure water. Drinking as much of it as you can is one of the fastest and easiest ways to sound better.

The reason why you have to drink so much water is simple. The salivary glands—the part of your body that creates phlegm—are at the very end of the line for water allocation in your body. When you drink, the vital organs get hydrated first in order to keep you alive. If there's any fluid left at the end, your vocal cords might get some. By overdrinking water, there's more than enough to cover all of the organs that need it and still allow the bloodstream to carry plenty to the cords.

And by the way, *phlegm* isn't a bad word. It's only a negative thing when it becomes so thick that it gets in the way of the cords' vibrating perfectly. The thin, watery type of phlegm is normal and necessary. If you didn't have enough of it, you wouldn't be able to speak at all, as it joins with the water and creates the ultimate lubrication for your voice.

The "No" List

Let's go down the list and figure out what we may need to avoid, reduce, or just know more about. My suggestion is that you read what I have to say, think about your own health choices, and then try to cut back on certain things as an experiment.

If you have to clear your throat quite a lot, get dry mouth regularly, or feel like there's always "stuff" in there, you need to take my advice seriously and be willing to make some changes. If you rarely clear your throat, have no real allergy issues, and seldom experience dry mouth, you can simply learn from the things I'm going to discuss next and consider yourself lucky. Either way, I won't ask you to go on bread and water alone; rather, I'd just like you to cut back on certain items to see if doing so makes you feel and sound better.

Dairy Products

Whenever I have a student who's always clearing his or her throat and dealing with way too much phlegm, the first thing I suggest is to eliminate dairy products from the diet. Milk, cheese, yogurt, and butter can create so much junk in your throat that it's difficult to speak through it.

Most of us were raised in a society that pushes dairy products as a necessary food group. Modern science, however, suggests that if you're more than ten years old, probably the less dairy, the better. I understand that it's a very common source of calcium and all of us need this mineral throughout our lives. Still, you could easily get enough of it from eating broccoli, and there's no negative attached.

Over the years, I've seen my students cut back on their dairy intake and watched as one by one, they dramatically benefited from doing so. I've heard scratchy, tired, hoarse voices change into strong, clear, healthy ones in no time at all. Think more seriously about your voice before you guzzle that tall glass of milk.

Caffeine

If you drink a lot of coffee, tea, or soda, chances are that you're consuming quite a bit of caffeine. Here's why that's a vocal problem: As I mentioned, caffeine acts as a diuretic and flushes water from your system. When you have less moisture, the mucous in your throat (that is, the phlegm) becomes more concentrated, which makes it harder to speak clearly and forces you to once again start clearing your throat. Caffeine creates dehydration by speeding up your whole metabolism. It stimulates the mucous-producing cells, and they work harder and faster to create unwanted levels of extra-thick phlegm.

I've had many a student claim that their life wouldn't be worth living without a morning cup of caffeinated coffee. To that I say, "All bad things in moderation." Have your morning cup, and then please switch to decaf or water for the rest of the day.

Carbonated Drinks

I've personally noticed over the years that the students who drink a lot of carbonated sodas usually have too much phlegm. Such beverages have a high level of acid. The combination of that acidity, the high sugar content, and the lack of any other health benefit makes soda a bad vocal choice. Besides, most people don't crave room-temperature soda . . . they only drink it if it's extremely cold. Based on what I've already taught you about the temperature of liquids, it's a double no-no.

Sugar

Some doctors believe that too much sugar can create thick phlegm, but there isn't a huge amount of evidence supporting that claim. It's certainly not as common a cause as dairy and caffeine. Still, everyone besides the Pillsbury Doughboy would probably agree that it's a great idea to limit how much sugar you eat. Your overall heath will improve, and your voice will be better because of it.

Citrus

People are always asking me about putting lemon in their tea because they've heard that it's a good thing. When I say that it's not, this usually catches them off guard. Here's what I believe: Citrus in the mouth makes you salivate, and extra saliva is a problem if it fills your mouth up with more than you want or need. Aside from that, citrus also creates phlegm that's way too thick. Drinking orange or grapefruit juice or lemonade creates a myriad of substances in your throat that you don't need to deal with.

As far as health reasons for drinking juice go, people are easily misled. Next to water, the most plentiful ingredient in the majority of the juices you buy is sugar or a sugar substitute. We already know that sugar is no good for you. Aside from that, there's evidence that fruit is only beneficial if you eat the whole individual fruit, such as one apple or orange. Doctors have reported that combining fruits changes their chemical composition, thereby lowering their nutritional benefits. I say go ahead and eat individual whole fruits for health reasons, but not within several hours of a really important conversation or presentation.

Red Meat

There's only so much blood in your body. When you eat red meat, your body sends a certain amount of that blood to your stomach and intestines to help digest the food. That takes it away from the muscles you use to speak, so there ends up being less blood and energy for the vocal cords. On days when you really need your voice, don't overdo the meat thing. That way, your body can concentrate on producing great sound, not breaking down difficult food.

Smoking

Although this chapter is about what to eat and drink, remember that all substances you take into your body can impact your voice. There are two holes in the throat: one for food and water and one for air. When you inhale anything, including cigarette smoke, it goes straight to the cords and instantly begins to dry up all the natural moisturizers that are lubricating them. Smoking is the one place where I have to draw the line: No amount of it is healthy for the cords. The only way to *love your voice* and *yourself* is to make the change and quit.

Alcohol

It's a medical fact that alcohol dehydrates the body, and that's not a good thing when you're trying to keep your vocal cords lubricated. My compromise is for you to limit your consumption to a maximum of two glasses of wine or a couple of beers, making sure that you have at least four to six hours for your body to break down the alcohol before you need to speak to somebody important.

Keep in mind that the less you weigh, the less tolerance for alcohol you have. And I never recommend hard liquor, because its alcohol content is way too high. An American beer may be between 3 and 5 percent alcohol, whereas 100-proof whiskey contains 50 percent—and that much can really dry out your vocal cords.

Gum

Many people think that chewing gum keeps their throat moist, but it doesn't—in fact, it does just the opposite. Gum is dry when it comes out of the pack, becomes moist when it's in your mouth, and then dries up when you take it out. So what do you think was keeping it moist? The answer is *saliva,* and that's not helping your speaking voice at all. The gum is using up a great deal of the saliva you need for speaking. My advice is to lose the gum, especially when you're getting ready to talk to somebody important.

Acid Reflux

There are only so many things that can traumatize the vocal cords, make them red and swollen, and get in the way of helping you sound fabulous. One is acid reflux, and millions of people suffer from this ailment. First, let me give you a brief definition, and then I'll suggest a few things you can do to combat the problem.

When you eat or drink something, the food or liquid reaches your stomach by passing through a tube called the esophagus. After it gets to your stomach, your body creates acid and a digestive enzyme called pepsin to break it down. While this is happening, your esophagus is supposed to be closed off so that nothing comes back up toward the throat. However, when this mechanism doesn't operate correctly, it can allow the contents of the stomach to "reflux" up the esophagus and into the throat. If you experience constant heartburn, a cough during the night, a bitter taste in your mouth, or frequent throat clearing, you might be dealing with reflux.

So let me offer a specific set of guidelines to help you cope with the problem. Some of these ideas are similar to what I've told you earlier in this chapter, but I also wanted to list them here under the specific category of acid reflux.

- Avoid spicy and acidic foods.

- Cut back on fruits, especially citrus; and fruit juices.

- Stay away from fatty foods such as chocolate.

- Limit your intake of coffee, tea, alcohol, and colas.

- Watch your weight, because being overweight increases abdominal pressure, which can aggravate the reflux.

- Don't gorge yourself at mealtime. Consume moderate amounts of food.

- Don't exercise too soon after eating.

- Avoid bedtime snacks, and eat meals three to four hours before going to sleep.

- Stop or cut down on smoking.

- Elevate the head of your bed with blocks or something similar.

The 10-Week Experiment

Now that I've had the opportunity to share a bit of semi-scientific dietary information, I'd like to offer you a relatively simple plan of action, a ten-week experimental program to help you create a diet that will work *for* you instead of against you. Most weeks, I'll ask you to eliminate a particular item and not consume it for the entire week. By the beginning of the third week, it should be clear whether or not you're receiving any benefits. If, for example, you eliminate food item *X* and find that during the week you're not clearing your throat as much, your voice seems to have more volume or resonance, or you just plain feel better, those would be positive results. If that happens, my advice is to eliminate that particular food item from your diet on a regular basis.

If for one reason or another, you're just not ready to make that commitment, at least try to cut way back on your consumption. Give it your best shot . . . anything you change for the better will move you in the right direction. Even if you only take small steps, you can still get to the finish line and complete the race. Good luck!

Week 1

I want you to start drinking four to six tall glasses of water a day. The water should be cool or room temperature. I don't want you to drink any that's been refrigerated or that has ice cubes mixed in. I'm okay with it if you want some of the water to be naturally carbonated. However, I still prefer that the majority be pure and noncarbonated. As soon as you get comfortable with drinking six glasses a day, I want you to up that number to eight. I understand that by consuming this much water you may need to visit the bathroom more frequently, but I know that the benefits will outweigh that particular inconvenience.

Week 2

Let's start out by eliminating the top-two food items related to extra-thick, unwanted phlegm: For one week, take milk and cheese out of your diet. I realize that this is a big thing to ask, especially if you enjoy a daily bowl of cereal for breakfast. Still, my goal is to offer you a better voice, a better ability to communicate, and then a better life. In order for that to happen, you need to be willing to try new things. I'm only asking you to start with one week. If you don't feel and sound better, you can go back to eating these foods.

During this first week, I don't even want you to substitute soy milk. Later on you can add it to your diet and see if it works for you. Many people react better to soy, and it could be a great alternative to the milk products . . . but not this week.

Week 3

This week I'd like you to continue eliminating dairy from your diet and lose the yogurt, ice cream, and butter. Hopefully your throat felt better and clearer after one week of not having milk and cheese. If so, please stay off those items and just add the yogurt, ice cream, and butter to the "no" list. If after Week 3, you don't

sound and feel better than you did at the end of Week 2, you can add small amounts of dairy back into your diet.

Week 4

At this point in your experiment, I'd like you to eliminate caffeine. Start reading the labels of everything you're drinking, and make sure that it doesn't contain any of this ingredient. By now you should be consuming eight glasses of water a day anyway, leaving very little drinking time for much else. But if you're still enjoying a morning cup of tea or coffee, please switch to herbal or decaf. Try it for one week: If you don't have less phlegm, aren't feeling any better, or are just going crazy without caffeine, add some back into your diet. Just remember that I'd like you to keep tabs on your consumption and never overdose on it ever again. It's not good for you or your voice.

Week 5

I'd like you to begin to eliminate some of the citrus you consume. Please do without that morning glass of orange or grapefruit juice. However, it's okay for you to have a whole orange once every other day. As I mentioned earlier, pieces of fresh fruit are always better for you than drinking a packaged mixture. My hope is that cutting down your citrus intake will give you a noticeable positive vocal change.

Week 6

The two best edible phlegm fighters are tomatoes and onions. I'd like you to start to regularly add those items into your diet. One of the easiest ways to do so is for you to have pasta with tomato sauce and onions a couple of times a week. If you'd rather not do the sauce approach, you can simply eat four or five raw tomatoes a week and add cooked onions into several other dishes you prepare.

Week 7

This week I'd like you to start eating dinner earlier in the evening. The later you eat, the harder it is for your body to digest the food. Snacking late and then going to sleep is very hard on the body. It's easy for the acid in your stomach to trickle up to the throat at night and make the vocal cords red and swollen.

Therefore, please have dinner by 7 and then don't eat anything after that. Not only will this help you vocally, it's also a wonderful way to lose any extra pounds you wanted to shed.

Week 8

This week is the perfect time to cut back on your alcohol consumption, especially late at night. Consume no hard liquor, and limit yourself to no more than two beers or glasses of wine for the entire week. Make sure that it's all before 7:30 P.M., as alcohol is difficult for the body to process when you drink it later in the evening and then go to sleep or otherwise remain fairly inactive.

Week 9

I'd like you to go an entire week without eating red meat and pay attention to how you feel and sound. As I've said, red meat is very difficult for the body to digest and deal with. I've seen people stop eating it and sound drastically better. Give it a try and see what happens.

Week 10

If you smoke any cigarettes, I want you to please stop. If that's more of a commitment than you're ready to make at this time, please cut back to almost none. If you don't smoke at all, make sure that this week you don't spend any time in smoke-filled areas or around people who are smoking. Secondhand smoke is still tough on the cords.

Give It Your Best Shot

Even though it's only a week at a time, I know that it's hard to do without some of your favorite food items. I still hope that you'll give my little experiment a try and see what it does for your throat. The goal is to provide a great deal of valuable information about which food items are or aren't causing extra unwanted, thick phlegm. Just give it your best shot, and don't drive yourself crazy or create unnecessary guilt. I'll take whatever positive progress I can get from you and then capitalize on that.

The Wrap-Up

Most people are walking around with mediocre voices. They plow through life dealing with whatever sounds happen to come out of their mouths, and they find it much harder to achieve the things they want and need. But the good news is, you're not one of those people anymore. You've made a genuine commitment to bettering yourself. You've boldly gone where most are afraid to tread. You took a good long look at the way you sounded and decided to make some changes.

You started with your breathing, making sure that the air was coming in and going out under your control (and please remember that your stomach still needs to be coming in the whole time you're speaking). You learned that there are actually three voices inside of you, and that the Middle voice is an important addition to a healthy and beautifully effective vocal range. You looked under your "hood" and did an engine overhaul by adding more melody and volume; and then you made sure that the speed, pitch, and tone of your voice were working for you. You looked into a mirror and became more aware of your hand gestures and body movements, eliminating the ones that were making you look physically uncomfortable. You examined your diet and you made some modifications to feel and sound better. For all of those changes and more, I'm extremely proud of you.

I've spent a great deal of my own life in the pursuit of vocal excellence. I realized as a toddler that voice was going to be a major theme for me. My parents told me stories of how I'd filled every waking moment of my early childhood with singing. I never quite understood why everyone around me was so hesitant about suddenly breaking into song and dance, but I believed then—and still do now—that it was their loss.

I sang in the school choir; performed in musicals; and studied guitar, piano, music theory, sight reading, and foreign languages (just in case I wanted to be an opera singer). I was already teaching voice by the time I was 13, and I became the younger partner in the most prestigious voice studio in Los Angeles by the age of 16. At 18, I was voted the number one solo voice in the state of California by the California Music Educators Association, before going on to UCLA as a voice major.

While working very hard to achieve my own personal sound goals, I was always excited about sharing my tools with others. Being a teacher has rewarded me with more incredible life experiences and lessons than I could ever count. I truly consider myself to be one of the luckiest people on Earth. Every single moment is filled with love, laughter, and music. When sadness does come sneaking in from around an unsuspected corner, it's easily defeated by any of those three things.

They say that great teachers learn a certain amount from their own teachers, but infinitely more from their students. I couldn't agree more. It's been my honor and pleasure to be *your* teacher. There's a world of new possibilities open for you now. When I say that a better life is waiting for you on the tip of your tongue, I mean it. Get out there and make a difference. Strive to make the world a better place, one voice at a time.

I'll be listening. . . .

Love,
Roger

CD Index

TRACK NUMBER	TITLE
Track 1	Demonstration: Chest, Middle, and Head Voice
Track 2	Exercise: "Goog" One Octave
Track 3	Exercise: "Mum" Low Larynx
	VOICE TYPES
Track 4	Demonstration: "The Nasal Professor"
Track 5	Demonstration: "The Rocky Balboa"
Track 6	Exercise: "Nay" One Octave
Track 7	Demonstration: "The Squeaky Hinge"
Track 8	Demonstration: "The Marilyn"
Track 9	Demonstration: "The Big Brass"
Track 10	Demonstration: "The Husky Voice"

BUILDING BLOCKS

Track 11	Demonstration: Volume
Track 12	Demonstration: Monotone
Track 13	Demonstration: Melody
Track 14	Demonstration: Pitch
Track 15	Demonstration: Tone
Track 16	Demonstration: Pace

VOCAL PROFILES

Track 17	Demonstration: Cashier
Track 18	Demonstration: Salesperson
Track 19	Demonstration: Doctor's Office
Track 20	Demonstration: Teacher
Track 21	Demonstration: Receptionist

DAILY WARM-UP

Track 22	Exercise: Female Warm-Up
Track 23	Exercise: Male Warm-Up

🎤 🎤 🎤

Acknowledgments

Every book I've written has a unique creation story and a special group of people to thank. The story of *Love Your Voice* begins with an unselfish gesture from a new friend, Monique Mallory, who introduced me to Reid and the entire Hay House family. For that I will remain forever grateful.

I'd also like to give a very special thank-you to Stacey Smith.

Reid Tracy—thank you for this wonderful opportunity and a new publishing adventure.

Jill Kramer—thank you for your guidance and support.

Alex Freemon—thank you for your suggestions and attention to detail.

B J Robbins—thank you for believing in my abilities as a writer and for stepping up to do something about it.

To my mother I say, "I love you and wish you were here to hear."

To my father I say, "I wrote this because you couldn't."

To my brother I say, "Cheer up; I still love you."

Dear Eiko and Jacques—thank you for parenting me when mine could no longer do it.

Jimmy—I'll call you when I need something.

Thank you to Tina, Alexa, Donat, Roger, and Ann.

The remainder of the people I wish to thank
will be forever in my heart but remain nameless here.

About the Author

Roger Love is recognized as one of the world's leading authorities on voice. He has vocally produced more than 100 million CDs worldwide; written two immensely popular books, *Set Your Voice Free* and *Sing Like the Stars!;* created the best-selling audio program *Vocal Power;* produced and starred in the DVD *Love to Sing;* and appeared as a regular in three major network TV shows: *Popstars* for the WB, *Rock Star: INXS* for CBS, and *The One: Making a Music Star* for ABC. Roger's work on the film *Walk the Line* resulted in three Golden Globe® Awards, a Grammy® Award, a Screen Actors Guild Award®, a platinum-selling CD award, and an Academy Award®.

Roger's singing students range from The Beach Boys to Eminem, and his acting clients include celebrities such as Reese Witherspoon and Joaquin Phoenix. He also instructs professional speakers such as Anthony Robbins and Suze Orman, as well as radio personalities such as Dr. Laura Schlessinger and Glenn Beck.

Website: **www.RogerLove.com**

Notes

Notes

Notes

Notes

HAY HOUSE TITLES OF RELATED INTEREST

BELIEVE IN YOURSELF, by Dr. Joseph Murphy

CREATING INNER HARMONY: Using Your Voice and Music to Heal, by Don Campbell (book-with-CD)

THE 8TH CHAKRA: What It Is and How It Can Transform Your Life, by Jude Currivan, Ph.D.

THE POWER OF INFINITE LOVE & GRATITUDE: An Evolutionary Journey to Awakening Your Spirit, by Dr. Darren R. Weissman

THE POWER OF PLEASURE: Maximizing Your Enjoyment for a Lifetime, by Douglas Weiss, Ph.D.

YOUR DESTINY SWITCH: Master Your Key Emotions, and Attract the Life of Your Dreams! by Peggy McColl

All of the above are available at your local bookstore, or may be ordered through Hay House (see next page).

We hope you enjoyed this Hay House book. If you'd like to receive
a free catalog featuring additional Hay House books and products, or
if you'd like information about the Hay Foundation, please contact:

Hay House, Inc.
P.O. Box 5100
Carlsbad, CA 92018-5100

(760) 431-7695 or **(800) 654-5126**
(760) 431-6948 (fax) or **(800) 650-5115 (fax)**
www.hayhouse.com® • **www.hayfoundation.org**

Published and distributed in Australia by: Hay House Australia Pty. Ltd.,
18/36 Ralph St., Alexandria NSW 2015 • *Phone:* 612-9669-4299
Fax: 612-9669-4144 • www.hayhouse.com.au

Published and distributed in the United Kingdom by: Hay House UK, Ltd.,
292B Kensal Rd., London W10 5BE • *Phone:* 44-20-8962-1230
Fax: 44-20-8962-1239 • www.hayhouse.co.uk

Published and distributed in the Republic of South Africa by: Hay House SA (Pty), Ltd.,
P.O. Box 990, Witkoppen 2068 • *Phone/Fax:* 27-11-706-6612 • orders@psdprom.co.za

Published in India by: Hay House Publishers India, Muskaan Complex,
Plot No. 3, B-2, Vasant Kunj, New Delhi 110 070 • *Phone:* 91-11-4176-1620
Fax: 91-11-4176-1630 • www.hayhouse.co.in

Distributed in Canada by: Raincoast, 9050 Shaughnessy St., Vancouver, B.C.
V6P 6E5 • *Phone:* (604) 323-7100 • *Fax:* (604) 323-2600 • www.raincoast.com

Tune in to **HayHouseRadio.com**® for the best in inspirational talk radio featuring
top Hay House authors! And, sign up via the Hay House USA Website to receive
the Hay House online newsletter and stay informed about what's going on wit'
your favorite authors. You'll receive bimonthly announcements about Discount'
Offers, Special Events, Product Highlights, Free Excerpts, Giveaways, and m'
www.hayhouse.com®